Poor Participation

Democratic Dilemmas and Policy Responsiveness

Series Editors: Thomas Bryer and Egle Butkeviciene

Public policy issues divide societies around the world, with resulting tensions that threaten the fabric of social cohesion and certain norms of empathy, compassion, and civility. Today, such hot button issues as poverty, refugee integration, immigration, and others are the source for implicit and explicit debate concerning the "fitness" and "worthiness" of some individuals and groups of individuals to be one with society. In social and democratic terms, some citizens are included-in and some are included-out. This series consists of books that address the democratic dilemmas that arise with desire to be responsive through policy to competing values, interests, and positions. Special attention will be given to local governance, where divisions often manifest most clearly, but works that address higher levels of government, as well as supranational governments, will also be included in the series. Accepted titles will be sole- or co-authored monographs or edited volumes, with emphasis on deep case analysis, comparative case studies, comparative empirical studies, or theoretical explorations.

Recent Title

Poor Participation: Fighting the Wars on Poverty and Impoverished Citizenship by Thomas A. Bryer and Sofia Prysmakova-Rivera

Poor Participation

*Fighting the Wars on Poverty and
Impoverished Citizenship*

Thomas A. Bryer and Sofia Prysmakova-Rivera

LEXINGTON BOOKS
Lanham • Boulder • New York • London

Published by Lexington Books
An imprint of The Rowman & Littlefield Publishing Group, Inc.
4501 Forbes Boulevard, Suite 200, Lanham, Maryland 20706
www.rowman.com

Unit A, Whitacre Mews, 26-34 Stannary Street, London SE11 4AB

British Library Cataloguing in Publication Information Available

Library of Congress Cataloging-in-Publication Data

Names: Bryer, Thomas A., 1978-, editor. | Prysmakova-Rivera, Sofia, author.
Title: Poor participation : fighting the wars on poverty and impoverished
   citizenship / Thomas A. Bryer and Sofia Prysmakova-Rivera.
Description: Lanham : Lexington Books, [2018] | Series: Democratic dilemmas
   and policy responsiveness | Includes bibliographical references and index.
Identifiers: LCCN 2018000240 (print) | LCCN 2017056655 (ebook)
Subjects: LCSH: Economic assistance, Domestic—United States. | Community
   organization—United States. | Community development—United States. |
   Citizenship—Moral and ethical aspects—United States.
Classification: LCC HC110.P63 (print) | LCC HC110.P63 B79 2017 (ebook) | DDC
   362.5/5610973—dc23
LC record available at https://lccn.loc.gov/2018000240

ISBN: 978-1-4985-3893-0 (cloth : alk. paper)
ISBN: 978-1-4985-3895-4 (pbk. alk. paper)
ISBN: 978-1-4985-3894-7 (electronic)

Contents

~

List of Figures

~

List of Tables

~

Preface

This book started with a guest lecture I gave at Chonnam National University in Gwangju, South Korea in 2014. The title of the lecture was "The War on Impoverished Citizenship: Reflections for Government-Citizen Relations around the Globe." It was an ambitious title and a topic that was a bit daunting given the history of that city. Starting on May 18, 1980, government troops killed upwards of 600 citizens following the shooting, beating, and killing of Chonnam National University students by military forces whilst they engaged in protest against the regime in power at that time. It was a humbling lecture to speak of democracy and public participation with government in a place where so many gave their lives in defense of democratic and participatory ideals.

Since that time, the work has taken new direction and new shape, informed by more contemporary world events between the period of 1980 and 2017. These events have demonstrated the complexity of citizenship, participation, democracy, and the real sacrifices that are necessary to create and empower stronger citizens and more responsive governments.

Events that carried a pulsation of change in the past nearly forty years include but are in no way limited to: the Baltic Way, shepherding the reclaimed independence of Estonia, Latvia, and Lithuania from the Soviet Union; collapse of the communist regime in Romania; Arab Spring rallies and protests that shook the power structures in Egypt and elsewhere; the Orange Revolution that gave voice to the masses in Ukraine; emergence of the Occupy movement in the United States and elsewhere, as well as the Black Lives

Matter movement; emergence of far-right and conservative movements and political parties, such as the Tea Party in the United States, United Kingdom Independence Party, Law and Justice Party in Poland, and others; increasingly complex migration patterns around the world, as individuals flee war, famine, oppression, and violence; and emergence of populist anxieties, the kind of which made political outcomes like Brexit and the Trump presidency possible. These are all, in their own unique way, presentations and representations of citizens who are eager for change, inclusion of their views and interests, and something approximating greater empowerment.

Sacrifices of citizens to appeal for freedom, justice, independence, fair treatment, and/or basic goods and services have included in these past decades minor and severe injury, disappearance and kidnapping, imprisonment, blacklisting, removal of passports for travel, social isolation, and death. Efforts to become empowered citizens have truly been moments, sometimes extended moments, of open war and, within some authoritarian states, covert war.

With this context and recognizing the great sacrifice of "ordinary" people around the world, we humbly offer this text—*Poor Participation: Fighting the Wars on Poverty and Impoverished Citizenship*. The title has double meaning. Our interest is the participation of the poor, and it is also the sorrowful state of participation of many, if not most, members of our societies. We aim to offer ideas, theories, principles, and practices to inspire thought if not action regarding efforts to reduce subsistence or material poverty in the United States (primarily) but also around the world. There are many more words that can be written on these topics, and many more have been; our goal with this text is to establish the framework for future research, theory development, and explorations of philosophical understanding.

The monograph is written as part of a series on *Democratic Dilemmas and Policy Responsiveness*. Throughout the text, we have suggested several dilemmas and conflicts, particularly around tensions between ideas of empowerment and manipulation, the individual and the collective, and groups of citizens that can be considered included-in or included-out from different aspects of society.

Finally, some parts of the text are written in first person singular ("I"). The book is a joint effort, but the primary author at times discusses personal anecdotes and reflections. In these cases, "I" refers to the primary author.

~

Acknowledgments

The concept for this book started with an invitation from Professor Hou-Gyun Kim to Thomas Bryer in 2014 to give a lecture at Chonnam National University in Gwangju, South Korea. The lecture was entitled "The War on Impoverished Citizenship: Reflections for Government-Citizen Relations around the Globe." Figure A.1 shows a photo of the banner created for this

Figure A.1. Acknowledgment of Chonnam National University

lecture. As such, the first expression of thanks must go to Professor Hou-Gyun Kim, students, and professors at Chonnam National University.

The themes and ideas developed for the lecture were subsequently expanded, tested, and presented in a variety of forums around the world, including during the annual public administration research conference at the University of Central Florida, an academic lunch seminar at Kaunas University of Technology in Lithuania, the European Group for Public Administration conference in The Netherlands, and in classrooms in various settings where students provided valuable feedback on the logic of argument. Without naming names, we are grateful to the many students, professors, and others who participated in these conferences, workshops, and lectures, and to the institutions that provided space for such open dialogue.

As with all projects, the preparation of a book requires time and thus time away from family. We thank our families, spouses, and children for ongoing support.

~

CHAPTER ONE

Poverty, Participation, and an Emergent New Path for the 21st Century

"Nothing about us without us is for us!" This is a popular phrase used within the process of implementing Poverty Truth Commissions in the United Kingdom (Downie 2016). Ultimately, the meaning of this catchy phrase is that decisions that are made about those living in poverty or near-poverty are illegitimate and quite possibly inadvisable and non-responsive to the needs and interests of the poor if the poor themselves are not involved in decision-making. Nothing about us without us is for us.

Yet, inside this intuitively appealing idea are a range of potential contradictions and conflicts. These conflicts are at the nexus between active citizenship and technical expertise, between promotion of stability in governance and empowerment of people, between empowerment that is genuine and sustainable and empowerment that is artificial, and between a "war on poverty" that is built on the ideas of collaborative governance and one that is built on an assumption of rule of the elite.

At the time of this writing, we stand approximately fifty years after the "beginning of the end" of the "war on poverty" launched in the United States by President Lyndon Johnson. This was a "war" that expanded existing programs and created new initiatives that aimed to fight not only the symptoms of poverty but poverty's causes. In a manner akin to history's great military leaders compelling their troops into a battle against long odds, where death to some if not most was a certain outcome, President Johnson sought to rally the Congress of the United States (Gillette 2010): "On many historic occasions the President has requested from Congress the authority to move against forces which were endangering the well-being of our country. This is such an occasion. On similar occasions in the past we have often been called upon to wage war against foreign enemies, which threatened our freedom. Today we are asked to declare war on a domestic enemy, which threatens the strength of our nation and the welfare of our people. If we now move forward against this enemy—if we can bring to the challenges of peace the same determination and strength which has brought us victory in war—then this day and this Congress will have won a secure and honorable place in the history of the nation, and the enduring gratitude of generations of Americans yet to come."

In 1967, the signs of a war not won became apparent, as the political alignments that made the Economic Opportunity Act of 1964 possible—the law that created the programs that would enable the frontline warriors to be deployed—shifted. The vision of an empowered citizenry taking control of their own fate, standing against entrenched interests in local government, prepared for community action facilitated through the maximum feasible participation of the poor, encountered a reality that brought the metaphor of "war" very close to full manifestation on city streets throughout the country (Cazenave 2007; Gillezeau 2010).

Though some impoverished citizens felt empowered, there was no universal empowerment. Though measures of material poverty and well-being improved, poverty in a multi-dimensional frame has remained as intractable an enemy as ever. The scourge of inequality continues to ravage terrain throughout the world and subjects near majorities of human beings to a life on earth of mere subsistence or less, such that pursuit of individual- or collective potential is thwarted and may never be seen as a dream worthy of the effort.

In the pages that follow in this chapter, we sketch the relationship between citizenship and poverty, and explore the tensions previously identified. At the heart of this discussion is an underlying premise: the poor are "left out" of the practice of full citizenship. Citizenship, like a swanky ball with a dress code, has an entryway that is blocked to those who do not align with the norms of society. Occasionally, the masses will storm the gates to demand attention; most prominently this is perhaps reflected in the Brexit vote in United Kingdom and election of Donald Trump to the presidency of the United States. As we will discuss, these occasional "intrusions" create instabilities that can reorient society and lead to healthy questioning of societal values, but they are destabilizing and potentially corrosive to sustainable governance, particularly if those who "stormed the gates" are not fully empowered within whatever new systems are constructed in the wake of their action. That is, if mass adversarial action is ultimately coopted by the same elite members of society, society will experience recurrences of disruption.

Dividing our societies into groups is part of the history of humanity, indeed of all animal species: the powerful and powerless, rich and poor, Christian and Jew and Muslim, omnivores and herbivores and carnivores, black and white and brown and yellow, gay and straight and bisexual, book smart and street smart, Democrat and Republican, man and woman and . . . other. The "other" is anyone who looks, speaks, worships, has marital or sexual relations with, eats, or otherwise behaves differently than "I" do. Fear of the "other" is grounded in concern for economic security, preservation of culture or language, preference for status quo living rather than forced change due to demographic shifts, and so on.

The poor are whom we can consider as "included-out" citizens. They are legally living in a place, but they are not afforded the same courtesies, entrusted with the same responsibilities, or respected in parallel processes as those citizens of greater means and who behave in manners that are more consistent with "middle class" values. This is a concept that emerged within the context of migration and immigration (Erni 2016), but it is equally applicable in analyzing the situation of the poor. These are citizens who may be encouraged to participate politically, but such participation may be observed with skepticism both by authorities and "included-in" citizens. Likewise, they may be encouraged to express their cultural or religious traditions, or they may be discouraged from doing so.

Poor citizens engaged in the "war on poverty" were part of what we could call the ground troops, and their progeny today, can be categorized as "included-out." When they started to emerge and force their agenda through adversarial action and social protest, they were questioned; their legitimacy was questioned; their aptitude was questioned; their willingness to work hard was questioned, and so on. As such, it is abundantly clear, and will be argued through this text, that citizenship and poverty are inextricably linked.

Citizenship and Poverty

Active, ethical citizenship is required in the development of interpersonal empathy, generalized social trust and felt belongingness. Alleviating poverty, or the conditions leading to or consequences of living in poverty, is more possible with empathetic, trusting, and community-oriented citizens. Attending to the substantive democratic needs of a society requires attention to the procedural democratic means of society, and vice versa simultaneously.

To win a war on poverty requires an equally strategic and aggressive war on impoverished citizenship.

However, there is a tension between government and citizens, and it is a tension that cannot easily be swept aside. This may be particularly true in the context of poverty relations when poverty is considered in three dimensions: subsistence, status, and agency.

Subsistence poverty occurs when an individual has an inadequate material resource, including food, money, housing, et cetera. Status poverty occurs when an individual is held in less regard compared to peers. Agency poverty "is nothing less than a condition in which those involved are prevented by material deprivation from engaging in self-constituting experiences of power and thus from maintaining themselves as subject" (Ci 2013, 334). The challenge, according to Ci (2013), is to maintain a separation between these forms of poverty and to particularly ensure that someone's lack of material well-being does not inevitably constrain them to a life absent power in political or governance processes. Government policy that deals with material well-being may not extend to and thus create adversarial relations with individuals suffering agency poverty.

The "war on poverty" had as a centerpiece the idea of "maximum feasible participation." This was an idea that was ill defined and thus subject to a range of interpretations and implementation strategies across the United States. Daniel Patrick Moynihan (1969) summarized four distinct conceptions of Maximum Feasible Participation: (1) *organize the power* structure by creating mechanisms for cooperation across existing government, nonprofit, and private sector organizations, (2) *expand the power* structure by developing opportunities for citizens with low income to enter the professional workforce, (3) *confront the power* structure by redistributing power through democratization processes, and (4) *assisting the power* structure by creating formal representation on boards or advisory councils for low-income citizens.

The dominant interpretation in the implementation of Maximum Feasible Participation perpetuated the government-versus-citizen relationship in the form of the third option: confront the power structure. However, the confrontation as implemented did not empower citizens; instead well-meaning but also financially well-off advocates for change effectively used the poor as pawns. As Melish summarizes (2010):

> The purpose of organizing was not to seek local solutions or to work cooperatively with local government on comprehensive, multisectoral anti-poverty plans with a variety of stakeholders. Rather, it was to instigate overloads in City and State welfare offices around the country, using legal mechanisms and

fixed-rights language in an effort to singularize a national response. In essence, the strategy flipped 'maximum feasible participation' on its head, and it used the War on Poverty's signature community action programs to do much of the heavy lifting.

In other words, impoverished citizens were told about their entitlements, such as minimum income, housing, nutritional food, and so on, and were organized to demand their entitlements from government offices. The effort effectively overwhelmed the social services systems in cities around the United States, which was the intent in order to facilitate new national level policy for protections of human rights and human dignity. The published goals of community action, specifically, emphasized self-sufficiency and community connections (Bunch and Suamoyo 2017).

This approach, however, failed to empower citizens, as it did not give voice and meaning of action to those with the least, as was the goal for at least some advocates as Attorney General Robert Kennedy states (1964, 7):

> The Community Action programs must basically change these organizations by building into the program real representation for the poor. This bill calls for maximum feasible participation of residents. This means the involvement of the poor in planning and implementing programs: giving them a real voice in their institutions.

Further, the approach effectively led to policy reactions that demonized the poor for demanding material goods without clearly demonstrating a willingness or desire to work. In terms of government-citizen relations, we might suggest that the impoverished never had a relationship with the government as citizens; their relationship was with individuals who claimed to represent them, and they in turn maintained an adversarial relationship with government. This arm's length relationship aligned with the philosophy expressed by the nation's founders: the people are not capable of representing their own interests directly, as they are driven more by passion than by reason.

Before proceeding to set the full parameters of the discussion, we introduce a different war: not on poverty but on citizenship. The battle, so to speak, will be to weaken the active weapons in this second war that perpetuate and make real the myth that citizens are not capable of reasonable thought and accurate representation of their own interests. Victory in this war will be reinvigorated or newly developed strong, sustainable, and skeptical but civil government-citizen relations.

Perhaps we call the victory a *rebirth of skepticism*, which is a play on the notion of a rebirth of democracy (Berry, Portney, and Thomson 1993). It is the idea that the "perfect" set of relations between government and citizen are not exemplified by unqualified trust and allegiant citizenship (Dalton and Welzel 2014). Instead, there needs to be some level of assertiveness, in which citizens openly question and pursue better responses to tough questions. Skepticism of this kind needs to be "reborn" given the state of government-citizen relations in the United States and throughout the world: the current state of affairs is one of distrust in all conditions. There is limited "suspension of judgment," leading not to assertive citizens but angry citizens prone more to mob action rather than deliberative discussion and action. A return to skepticism as a goal is the victory we should seek.

Within this context—the war on the poor, the war on (impoverished) citizenship, the war on poverty, and the war for skepticism—the battles will be on the following fronts: (1) expertise versus mass competence, (2) transparency versus informed judgment, (3) volunteers versus active citizens with the state, (4) consumerism versus citizenship, (5) quantity versus quality, (6) representation versus inclusivity, and (7) tolerance of ignorance through manipulation versus empowerment.

These battlefronts will guide towards a recommended Maximum Feasible Participation (MFP) for the 21st century, or a Maximum Empowerment Participation (MEP). This updated model is inclusive and capable of addressing not only "traditional" poverty but also the poverties associated with modern day crises, such as the refugee situation in the United States and Europe.

To be sure, we are not interested in empowerment by granting political power to the masses, poor and non-poor, who can increase ability to subsist despite their ignorance. Genuine empowerment requires information and the ability to interpret the actions of others in the context of one's own self-interest. We are not interested in empowering ignorance, nor are we interested in ignoring the powerful by giving new voice to the powerless. We place our work at the nexus of multiple centuries of philosophy and policy directed at poverty: it is personal and collective, economic and social, concerning freedom and responsibility, adversarial and consensual, justice and beneficence. The context of this nexus is summarized in a historical review of poverty policies (Ravallion 2013, 79):

> This paper has tried to describe and better understand how the idea of antipoverty policy emerged and evolved over the last 200 or more years. It has been argued that we have transited between two radically different views of poverty. In the first, there was little reason to think that poor people had the potential to be anything else than poor. Poverty would inevitably persist, and was indeed deemed necessary for economic expansion, which required a large number of

people eager for work, and avoiding hunger was seen as the necessary incentive for doing that work.

Social policy had a role in assuring social stability—most importantly, a generally docile working class willing to work for low wages—and successfully so it seems in the case of England's Poor Laws. Promotional antipoverty policies would probably not have made much sense to those in power, although the need for protection from shocks would have been more evident, and appears to have had reasonably broad support from the elites even when mass poverty was taken for granted. However, beyond short-term palliatives to address shocks, there was little or no perceived scope for public effort to permanently reduce poverty. And a world free of poverty was unimaginable—after all, who then would be available to farm the land, work the factories and staff the armies?

In the second, modern, view, poverty is not only seen as a social ill that can be avoided through public action, but doing so is seen as perfectly consistent with a robust growing economy and indeed the right antipoverty policies are expected to contribute to that growth by removing material constraints on the freedom of individuals to pursue their own interests. In short, antipoverty policy came to be quite widely seen as an important element of the "social commitment to individual freedom." (Sen 1999, 284)

In short our interest is in seeing and treating poverty as a concern of democracy. Even with the change in rhetoric that suggests poverty is solvable throughout the world, in practice, the solutions have perpetuated the view that poverty is a necessary and acceptable condition. The extent of impoverished citizenship for the whole population and the lack of genuine empowerment of the poor has allowed the poor, undereducated and denied equal social standing, to be manipulated in politics. Elite political actors use the poor to pursue their interests, without enabling the poor to hold them to account. The representation link is broken, and a permanent lower-class persists. Poverty persists not for economic necessity but for political expediency. To solve poverty, to fight an active and effective war on poverty, requires more than meeting material needs with cash and non-cash assistance; it requires genuine empowerment and a relief in equal measure of poverties of agency and status.

We focus much of our discussion and launch our consideration of a path forward from the 1960s when we witnessed one of the first national concerted efforts to eliminate poverty and not just treat the impoverished. This is a legacy on which we aim to build, as it is fresh in the collective consciousness and newly debated as we sit a short distance from the 50th anniversary of the launch of the War on Poverty and close to the 30th anniversary when President Ronald Reagan declared in his 1988 State of the Union address that poverty won.

War on Poverty, Maximum Feasible Participation, and Possible Reformulation

Tara Melish (2010) was one of the first to systematically review the War on Poverty and most specifically MFP and suggest how the idea could be improved using governance innovation over the past fifty years. As summarized by Melish (2010), President Lyndon Johnson constructed the theory and operationalization of War on Poverty programs within the foundation of what he called "creative federalism." As a practice of federalism or intergovernmental relations (IGR), this creativity represented a departure from other forms of federal-state-local relations. Creative federalism required, to a certain extent, the abandonment of certain perhaps reified relationships that became rigid and non-adaptive. These relationships had to be reconfigured from the bottom-up and top-down simultaneously, at least in the manner envisioned by Johnson.

This "creative federalism" was a continuation of a tradition in IGR within the United States to adapt the role of the federal government to emergent societal needs. The philosophy assumed that a single federal solution to complex social and economic problems is not possible and not responsive to context-specific community needs. Perhaps ironically, often this adapted role enabled the federal government to assume more power over domestic policy, in the form of financial incentives, regulatory coercion, or through the blending of duties across levels of government. Though the precise prescriptions might not have been specified, the more free movement of money allowed values of the administration in Washington, DC to seep into the daily existence and practice of local governments, sometimes without the direct involvement of local government officials. Creativity came in the form of a dismantling of intergovernmental layers.

Popular with students of IGR are cake metaphors. A layer cake symbolized the relationship between levels of government in early American history, as a clear separation with distinct and defined duties. Creative federalism can be symbolized as a marble cake, in which boundaries are blurred, and distinct areas of responsibility are confused, at worst, or shared, at best. As the federal government expanded its powers with creeping activity in areas originally established within the purview of state and local governments, the cake that symbolized best also flipped. The pineapple upside down cake is heavy on top, light on bottom.

Previewing some of our future discussion, a new cake symbol has emerged in recent years that aligns with the "new accountability" and governance frameworks described by Melish. The multi-flavored wedding cake symbolizes the "extra-state" federalism characterized by collaborations, networks, and partnerships that span public, private, academic, and faith sectors (see discussion in Bryer 2014b).

As such, and in agreement with Melish, we can suggest that the institutional environment is dramatically and substantively different today as compared to the creative federalism of the 1960s. In the ensuing decades, the federal government has developed and used new financial tools to incentivize or coerce state and local governments to act in certain ways; it has taken pages from philanthropic and private sector playbooks to create competition within government, between government and private actors, between private companies, and across sectors; and, it has through its grant-making process established incentives for the development of cross-sector partnerships and networks.

The tool chest that exists today to implement "creative federalism" is more robust, more refined, and more attuned to the specific sector-based interests that exist in communities throughout the country. However, the boundaries of the creativity go well beyond IGR; the environment today is very much one of "extra-state" federalism, making the multi-flavored wedding cake an ideal metaphor. Multiple flavors reflecting the multiple sectors and interests are increasingly entering relationships with each other that are cooperative, coordinated, and sometimes fully collaborative—just shy of "marriage."

Melish suggests within this new environment that the same dual perspective or dual mandate that President Johnson envisioned—national entitlement programs combined with community action programs with MFP—are what should guide a 21st century war on poverty. As she writes, "The challenge is how to tie these two components together in a national orchestrating structure, ensuring that the practical obstacles, lessons, and solutions identified at the local level by intended beneficiaries can in fact be channeled effectively to influence, in a regular manner, the design and modification of targeted anti-poverty programs at local, state, and national levels" (2010, 7).

The idea of "national orchestration" is one that requires additional attention. Insofar as we are no longer operating within a strict environment of "creative federalism" but of extra-state federalism, national orchestration may be anathema to the very stakeholders who have innovation capacity, and human, social, and financial capital to wage a war on the multiple sources of the multiple manifestations of poverty—subsistence, agency, and status—and poor citizenship. In other words, national orchestration that seeks to monitor, coordinate, and/or direct local activities can serve as an institutional "psychological" barrier to innovate.

Whether intended or not, a national orchestration plan has the potential to enact actual or perceived (which is just as consequential as actual) manipulation. As Melish observes, during the 1960s implementations of community action and MFP, the poor themselves were not empowered; they were more manipulated and used almost as pawns by well-meaning elites coming into communities from outside. The same fate is perhaps highly likely for any anti-poverty set of initiatives that have at their center national coordination and orchestration, and are founded on assumptions of subsistence entitlements rather than genuine empowerment.

Entitlements themselves are perceived negatively in popular media; the Personal Responsibility and Work Opportunity Reconciliation Act signed by President Bill Clinton and policy proposals made by Republican policy leaders in Congress and in the Trump administration today have effectively rendered the very basic idea of entitlement to be dead on arrival. Political rhetoric of today, combined with the institutional capacities that have been developed and tested in the past fifty years point towards an alternative.

Melish (2010) suggests MFP can be resurrected in better form today given advancements in theory and practice related to new governance and new accountability that rely on decentralization and collaboration integrated with performance measurement and management. At the heart of Melish's proposal is a set of values that are consistent with Ci's (2013) admonishment that agency poverty not be subjugated to subsistence poverty. Melish writes (2010, 15): "[The poor] wish to reclaim a space for themselves, to cast off notions of their 'inability' or 'dependence,' and instead compel the public and government actor to see them as human beings with dignity, agency, and a drive to be treated on the basis of equal opportunity—not charity or paternalism."

In July 2017, an official with the Democrat Party of Florida echoed the same basic idea but in a way not so artfully constructed and with an eye towards partisan political advantage, thus leading to the official making an apology. The official suggested that the poor are emotional beings with great needs and thus act emotionally, sometimes in opposition to what the non-poor party official sees as being within their interests from a policy perspective. The official said: "[The poor are] emotional beings who are struggling to make a living, and they need to know that somebody's going to be on their side and be able to help them" (Miami Herald Editorial Board 2017). Her meaning was that the poor will not vote during elections based on issues but based on emotion, potentially emotional manipulation. Her argument was essentially that the poor can be manipulated based on the appearance of caring, and this is more important for the party than addressing issues. The *lack* of agency, or the high agency poverty, is a partisan political tool. As such, Melish and Ci's argument has credence; agency poverty cannot be ignored.

Melish's proposal further centers on a set of "organizational precepts and guiding principles" (2010, 11): "These include a shared policy preference for decentralization and broad stakeholder participation, flexible results-oriented policy planning, coordinated public-private partnerships, innovation and competitive experimentalism, rigorous monitoring and performance evaluation, and nationally-orchestrated incentive systems around defined performance goals and targets" (2010, 11). To achieve these aims, Melish suggests the creation of "orchestrating" bodies operating across the national landscape. One is a National Office on Poverty Alleviation, which would reside in the Executive Office of the President and serve to coordinate the various components of social welfare and anti-poverty programming. Second is a National Human Rights Commission, which would be "required to ensure that transparent monitoring processes were being independently undertaken around the nation on the impact of government policies on human rights, particularly of the most disadvantaged" (2014, 126).

These agencies would be guided by National Poverty Reduction Targets that, for instance, set a goal for reducing poverty by 50 percent over ten years. The concept here is straightforward: to draw attention to issues of poverty, there needs to be not only clearly stated goals but mechanisms for tracking movement toward goal accomplishment.

Within this context, Melish proposes "broad stakeholder responsibility and participatory commitments" that require the MFP of "all stakeholders in society, operating in increasingly broad community partnerships" (2010, 117). She continues, "such partnerships seek to take advantage of the full scope of human, financial, technological, and informational resources available, from the dense knowledge and expertise in local communities of poverty's causes, to the entrepreneurial skills, ideas, and investment potential of private business, to the civic energies of private citizens, to the research capabilities of the nation's universities and educational institutions" (2010, 117–118).

On the whole, these are sound recommendations, but they fall short on two major counts: (1) they ignore Ci's (2013) conception of agency poverty and focus on subsistence poverty, and (2) related, in focusing MFP on a broad class of stakeholders, they do not provide sufficient attention on the individual in poverty and his or her need for agency renewal and self-empowerment. As Ci argues, there must be a "severing of any links that happen to exist between socially valued forms of agency on the one hand and levels of income on the other, so that agency can no longer be undermined by low levels of income" (2013, 141). Failure to pay heed to agency poverty and to establish "targets" for empowerment in conjunction with poverty reduction targets will potentially further alienate those in poverty and reify the social and political divisions between those who have income-agency and those who do not, despite the best effort at MFP of a broad class of stakeholders.

We can use Melish's structure as a base but must enhance its democratic foundation, as well as the foundation of collaborative governance. The systems and processes we recommend are grounded in a set of distinct but related conceptions of poverty, participation, and empowerment. Each conception revolves around the twin issues of citizenship and its meanings, and empowerment in multiple forms.

The objective of the alternative is empowerment through reduction first of agency and status poverty, while meeting subsistence needs sustainably. There are two paths, building on but going beyond Melish's conceptual framework. The first interprets the goal of MFP as a process of what Moynihan (1969) defines as "organizing" the power structure. Melish (2010) follows closely with the label "institutional cooperation," defined as "the cooperative division of labor between stakeholders at all levels of society, all designed to assist government in the common consensual project of poverty alleviation." The second is focused on direct engagement of the poor in decision-making, both from outside and inside, or "confronting" and "assisting" the power structure, to use Moynihan's language.

Outline for the Remainder of the Book

Figure 1.1 displays the core concepts that form the basis of the arguments presented throughout the book. These will be unpacked in the chapters that follow. Suffice to say now that there are understood to be three kinds of citizens (included-in, included-out, and excluded), coupled with three forms of citizenship (ethical/political, cultural/religious, and legal) each at high and low levels, and dispersed across citizens experiencing different degrees of agency and status poverty. Available participatory strategies span the fine line between empowerment and manipulation, with the opportunity for outright exclusion reserved particularly for those citizens who are considered to

Included-In Citizen	Included-Out Citizen	Excluded Citizen
Low Agency Poverty	High Agency Poverty	High Agency Poverty
Low Status Poverty	High Status Poverty	High Status Poverty
High Ethical/Political Citizenship	Low Ethical/Political Citizenship	Low Ethical/Political Citizenship
High Legal Citizenship	Low Legal Citizenship	Low Legal Citizenship
High Cultural/Religious Citizenship	Low Cultural/Religious Citizenship	Low Cultural/Religious Citizenship
Empowered Participation	*Manipulated Participation*	*No Participation*
Mobilization	Cooptation	Exclusion
Persuasion		

Subsistence Poverty

Figure 1.1.   War on Poor Citizenship Concept Map

be deviants. All of these factors combine in multiple patterns to affect the subsistence poverty struggles faced by individuals at any one time, and the subsistence poverty that can plague whole societies over time.

In chapter 2, we look in more detail at one component of the slogan introduced in the opening sentence of this chapter: Nothing about us without us is for us. Specifically, we consider the question: Who is "us"? In other words, who are the poor, in the context of all three forms of poverty (subsistence, status, and agency), across different geographies (urban, rural, and suburban). In this chapter, we present not only data from a variety of objective sources but will demonstrate the complexity of poverty data by introducing mini-case examples drawn from popular media.

The third chapter focuses on the other component of the slogan. Specifically, what does it mean for policymaking and implementation to be "without" us or the opposite "with" us? Here we will spend much more time analyzing the meanings of MFP, as it was developed in the 1960s United States and how it is still interpreted today. Referring to the concept map (figure 1.1), whereas chapter 2 contains explication of the kinds of poverty, chapter 3 emphasizes forms of citizenship as a means to distinguish inclusion from exclusion in society.

In the fourth chapter, we build on a theme introduced in the third chapter and assess assumptions regarding the capacity of individuals and collectives to represent self and represent other. Are those experiencing poverty the best to represent their own interests? Are those who have never experienced poverty capable of addressing the needs and advocating for the interests of the poor? The lines between included-in, included-out, and excluded citizens will be made at once clear within this chapter but also potentially muddled as the subjectivity of who belongs in what category will be identified as one of the critical issues preventing a societal "attack" on poverty in all of its forms.

Chapter 5 drives us towards the next steps in efforts to fight poverty, beginning with a clear articulation of past anti-poverty efforts. Both historical texts and contemporary critiques will be synthesized, including a recently published oral history about the development of War on Poverty programs, fifty-year retrospectives published by the Budget Committee of the U.S. House of Representatives and by the White House, and other academic and legal texts. A central critique that is advanced in this chapter is that the potential of War on Poverty programs was not realized due to the failure to empower those who are poor. In other words, the programs targeted subsistence poverty without addressing agency and status poverty and without considering citizens and citizenship holistically.

Chapter 6 presents a more in depth and theoretical review of one anti-poverty program in the United States: Community Development Block Grant program. We select this as an ideal program for review given its near genesis in original War on Poverty programs, its shifts in character and focus during the past decades, and the current political battles regarding its continued existence. The case provides opportunity to understand the complexity of anti-poverty efforts that seek to combine a national mechanism with local discretion. We discuss proposed anti-poverty policies in the United States for the 21st century in this chapter as well, with particular focus on suggestions from the early days of the Trump administration in the United States.

In chapter 7, we present our own solution for fighting a war on poverty and poor participation in the 21st century. As previously indicated, it is a "war" that will be addressed on multiple fronts: (1) expertise versus mass competence, (2) transparency versus informed judgment, (3) volunteers versus active citizens with the state, (4) consumerism versus citizenship, (5) quantity versus quality, (6) representation versus inclusivity, and (7) tolerance of ignorance through manipulation versus empowerment.

Chapter 8 applies the logic presented in the seventh chapter to separate but related policy areas that are challenged with the same variables: refugees and refugee integration, and homelessness. We consider how our solution for a new "war on poverty and impoverished citizenship" can lead potentially to more seamless democratic, cultural, and economic integration of refugees in communities particularly in the United States and Europe. This chapter also particularly serves to emphasize the importance of a clear "organize the power structure" framework to forge sustainable cross-sector relationships in police development and intervention.

In the ninth chapter, we consider policies in comparison nations, specifically focusing on new laws in the Netherlands, basic income experiments in Finland and elsewhere, and struggles with poverty in the post-Soviet space of Lithuania. These examples, held in comparison against each other and with the United States, provide fresh insight to the ideas established in the seventh chapter.

The conclusion will summarize key arguments and suggest future research directions. Let the battles begin.

CHAPTER TWO

~

About "Us"

Defining who the poor are is an act of scientific objectivity, subjective self-identification, and inter-subjective concurrence across individuals in a society. The task is more difficult still when applying differential costs of living across place and when seeking to apply normative understandings of "deserving" and "undeserving" poor. In this chapter, we cover the full territory, asking: who are the poor, in the context of all three forms of poverty (subsistence, status, and agency), and across different geographies (urban, rural, and suburban)? We will review the scientific objective measures as well as delve into the subjective and inter-subjective realities of poverty and life in poverty.

To begin, we can define poverty as something that is experienced. It is lived. To place our subjective bias in plain view, neither of us, the authors, have lived in poverty, according to any of the definitions that are outlined here. We have endured the "hardship" of graduate school subsistence, but within this context, we have had supportive family, access to transportation, access to nutritious foods, and access to money—either our own or someone else's.

In February 2017, I participated in a poverty simulation.[1] In this process, participants are randomly assigned a role of a parent, child, single-adult, with mixed situations, including various conditions of employment, health, housing, and financial reserve. My random assignment was as an eight-year-old boy, with an older sister and younger brother, plus two parents, both unemployed. Every thirteen or so minutes represented a week in the life of the family, and we had to "very simply" try to survive. As a child, I was sent to school each week and did not experience the full pressure of trying to get access to services of various kinds, but my "protected" world crashed around me when my parents said, "we have not had any food in three weeks." As a role-play exercise, this realization was stressful for me, and for the remainder of the exercise, I genuinely could not focus on my life as a child.

I developed another simulation exercise, without the complex character portrayals. Whereas the Poverty Simulation embeds deep character, forces strategic decision-making and moral compromise, my exercise focuses on the general frustration of seeking access to all the care a person in poverty requires—job training, healthcare, education, drug rehabilitation, and so on. Participants divide into groups of three or four, and move from place to place, based on instructions left at eighteen different stations. On their journey, participants unwind a pack of colored yarn and tape it to the wall at each place they go. The end result, with four or more groups working simultaneously, is a room covered with yarn, crossing in random pathways. The lesson: where one enters the social service delivery system, a potentially "random" choice, will alter the path they travel and their likely success getting all of their needs met. Figure 2.1 shows a photograph from one such exercise.

These exercises, conducted in the safety of a classroom or community center, help raise awareness of unique conditions. They help participants feel the frustration, thus potentially creating increased empathy (a subject to which we will return in the third and fourth chapters), but they are too small-scale to shift inter-subjective impressions of poverty and the poor within the broader society. Further, after experiencing the "trauma" of being poor for a couple of hours, participants in these kinds of exercises, will end the session with a well-balanced meal and/or a $5 latte at the nearest coffee house.

Definitions of Poverty

Poverty is a complex and multidimensional phenomenon, shaped by age, gender, culture and race, and the geopolitical and economic context of the place where the poor live (Ferragina, Tomlinson, and Walker 2013; Elmelech and Lu 2004). The concept of poverty has many definitions and interpretations as well as causes. From a political science perspective, poverty is a lack of power and equal access to goods and services. Economists tend to believe that poverty is a lack of resources. Money, employment, housing, and education are among the main solutions to the issue (Gillette 2010). Sociologists assume that people bring their own purposes to the poverty question, which makes poverty a "very deep-rooted social, psychological, attitudinal, value-

Figure 2.1. Simulating Poverty

laden concept" (Gillette 2010, 6). According to Narayan-Parker and Patel (2000) poverty is an interlocked, psychological concept. The lack of access to infrastructure, literacy, and the inability of the impoverished to cope with vulnerability and poor health are the main causes of poverty.

Ci (2013) also differentiates between three types of poverty: subsistence, status, and agency. Subsistence poverty is a lack of resources, caused by unemployment and often a low level of education. Status poverty is shaped by public perceptions and stereotypes about impoverished people, often defined through media and political rhetoric. Agency poverty is defined by a lack of one's capacity for free choice and action. Status deprivation makes people feel powerless, which consequently leads to agency poverty (Ci 2013). Status and agency poverty prohibit impoverished people from being engaged in civil society activities and decision-making processes that address needs in their communities (Pogge 2009).

Communities with higher proportions of ethnic and racial minorities often find themselves being economically segregated, discriminated against, and denied fair treatment in educational and employment opportunities (Dreier, Mollenkopf, and Swanstrom 2014). According to critical race theory, poverty and race intersect in many ways. Although there is a general perception that recipients of welfare are mostly "black and brown faces . . . more whites receive welfare than do people of color" (Delgado and Stefancic 2017, 123).

Even with that being the case, "African Americans are much less likely to succeed even holding multiple parental status variables constant . . . on average, blacks experience less upward mobility and whites less downward mobility" (Smeeding 2016, 107). Perhaps the most striking statistic to demonstrate this gap is that approximately 50 percent of black children born into the bottom 20 percent of income distribution remain in that income bracket as an adult, whereas only 23 percent of white children born into the lower tier of income remain so in adulthood. This gap, Smeeding (2016) suggests, is explained by factors such as parental occupation status, individual educational attainment, and marital status.

However, according to Dreier et al. (2014), racial segregation cannot be the only cause of poverty. In the past four decades, racial segregation has decreased, however, economic segregation has increased. The high level of divergence occurred between low and high-income people. Before Lyndon Johnson launched the War on Poverty, poverty had been mostly concentrated in inner cities, where ethnic minorities reside. In the last four decades, the poverty rate has significantly increased in suburbs where higher proportions of white people reside (Kneebone and Berube 2013).

Before we report additional objective data on poverty, we examine the individual subjective and the societal inter-subjective perceptions of poverty and the poor. These are the stories that shape societal consciousness, both potentially creating a heartfelt desire to help or a tough love mentality to leave the individual in poverty to pull him or herself up with hard work despite the odds and fragmented social service delivery system.

Self- and Other-Perceptions of Poverty

Schneider and Ingram (1997) categorize groups of people in a policy-making context as powerful/not powerful and deserving/undeserving. The (subsistence) poor are without power; they have no surplus time, material or financial resources to invest in the effort of lobbying government officials in any sustained way. Some of the poor may be deemed more deserving of support than others; for instance, homeless veterans, single working mothers, and hungry children. These are what Schneider and Ingram label "dependents." On the other hand, "deviants" are powerless and undeserving, at least in perception, such as drug and alcohol addicts, able-bodied unemployed, and so on. Policymakers may be rewarded for their efforts to help dependents and their efforts to erect more burdens and barriers for deviants to overcome; they may be politically harmed if they are seen to help deviants.

This intuitively appealing classification system, however, does not always hold. Though citizens might feel certain sympathy for hungry children, to be a hungry child or homeless child within a school where peers are housed and fed, establishes a stigma. To be a recipient of social support/welfare and be required to take a drug test before receiving benefits has been challenged as an invasion of privacy. Yet, in the latter case, the perception of the deviant remains for many policymakers and fellow citizens, stereotypes regarding the work ethic of the poor and drug habits of the impoverished.

An episode of the PBS television series, *Frontline*, aired in 2017 that revealed some of these perceptions. The episode, entitled "Poverty, Politics, and Profit" (see http://www.pbs.org/wgbh/frontline/film/poverty-politics -and-profit/), focused overall on the business side of public housing and how certain entrepreneurs have established lucrative careers by producing and developing housing for the poor. Part of the narrative focused as well on public perception of public housing and the people who required such housing.

One woman was interviewed about a proposed public housing community that would be developed next to her neighborhood. Identified as an opponent to the project, she describes how "the lifestyle that goes with Section 8 is usually working single moms or people struggling to keep their heads above water. It is not people who are the same class as us." She goes on to describe how she has heard critique of her position that those who cannot live in a good neighborhood will not be afforded certain opportunities. As someone who appears to be comfortable financially, she does not covet the resources and more exceptional opportunities of the super rich. The poor, she suggests, should be the same. "I am definitely not a racist. I am not a bigot. I think I hold a little bit of a stigma against people who are different. We don't want nomads who have no roots. I don't want this to be what our community is about."

In the context of the United States, a strong cultural orientation grounded in the idea of the rugged individual creates a view of those who are not successfully able to pull themselves up and thrive as lazy and deserving of whatever hardships they endure. Rosenblatt (1984, para. 1) summarizes this mystique:

> More aggressive than mere individuality, less narcissistic than the "me" decade, it does not refer to people who live in health clubs or on roller skates, or to the hotly cultivated yuppies who have come to mean so much to themselves. The "rugged" saves "rugged individualism" from shabbiness by implying not merely solitary but courageous action. Look. Here comes America. Davy Crockett. Thomas Edison. Teddy Roosevelt. Henry Ford. Those fellows built a nation with their hands.

Acting in any way outside of this cultural expectation carries with it a stigma, a shot against status in the community, regardless of extenuating circumstances that might have given rise to poverty. White (2009, 20) discusses this phenomenon within the context of the housing crisis in 2008 and beyond:

> People are less likely to default if doing so will make them feel like immoral or irresponsible persons—and are especially unlikely to default if they believe others will think of them as immoral or irresponsible persons. Guilt and shame are powerful motivators, and there is no doubt that many people who have faced foreclosure feel a great deal of both. As Linda, a single mom in Tampa who asked that her last name not be used, explained, "As a mom, I fee like I let my children down . . . It's a terrible embarrassment, and it's humiliating." Linda is not alone: a recent qualitative sociological study of the internal costs of foreclosure found that feelings of personal failure, shame, and embarrassment dominated the accounts of individuals who had lost their homes to foreclosure. Moreover, such feelings predominated even when individuals were not at fault for their predicament, but were victims of the declining economy and/or unethical practices by mortgage brokers.

These self- and other-perceptions matter and can lead to an even more vicious cycle than the impoverished condition does alone. As Bryer notes (2012, 306):

> Inner tension can be created when the public world of yard work and play is kept separate from the kitchen table conversations of financial distress. Fear of being labeled immoral or irresponsible may push individuals or families into further distress caused by their not asking for help or by their keeping up appearances with all the requisite spending habits of the financially responsible family. It is perhaps ironic then, that should a family slip into foreclosure, its

name is published for the world to see in local newspapers. By that time, of course, it is too late to receive the community support that might have allowed a family to resolve at least some of its financial dilemma.

The negative self-image coupled with the negative image imposed by others establishes the foundation of a vicious cycle of agency and status poverty, feeding off each other, and consequently preventing subsistence poverty from being addressed in a meaningful way. Perceptions matter for individual lives and for policymakers intent on manipulating lives for better or worse.

For instance, United States Representative Jason Chaffetz suggests the poor do not have appropriate priorities, choosing "frivolous" purchases like an iPhone instead of investing in healthcare. This is a view, as Pimpare (2017, 2) notes, that has an underlying assumption that "people would not be poor if only they would try harder." A review of recent op-ed and regular articles from the *Washington Post* suggest this kind of assumption is prevalent:

- Stop blaming poor parents for their children's limited vocabulary (Thomas 2014)
- This is what happened when I drove my Mercedes to pick up food stamps (Cunha 2014)
- We are overmedicating America's poorest kids (Rappaport 2014)
- American policy fails at reducing child poverty because it aims to fix the poor (Cohen 2017)

The negative perceptions of the poor are not new. Indeed, the words have changed, but the underlying sentiment has remained largely the same. The underlying assumption, as Pimpare writes (2017, 2), is that the "United States is a land of opportunity, where upward mobility is readily available and hard work gets you ahead." This is the *achievement ideology* that exists mostly for those who have the tools necessary to achieve (MacLeod 2009). For those who grow up in an impoverished situation, they may not readily "buy into" the achievement ideology: with hard work, I too can succeed.

Historically, over time and across societies the poor have been labeled in such ways as to create a feeling of inadequacy (Trattner 1994). Quoting extensively from Gans (1995):

The largest number of labels seems to have been invented for the various kinds of poor people deemed defective. These include, again in approximate historical order: paupers (as shiftless); debauched; hopeless classes; "ne'er-do-wells"; dregs; residue; residuum; feebleminded; morons; white trash; school dropouts; culturally deprived or disadvantaged; and poor in culture of poverty.

To this list must be added the class of labels that view the defective poor as dangers to public health, referring to their ragged and dirty state, their living in slums, and the like. This set of labels was particularly important before and during the nineteenth century, although some overtones of past labels survive in today's AIDS victims and needle-using substance-users. The delinquents include the politically threatening: the dangerous classes, Lumpenprolezariat, and sometimes, rabble and mob.

Charles Loring Brace used the term "dangerous class" in America for homeless children, also called street urchins or street arabs, because he feared what they would do politically when they were adults. The remainder of the labels for delinquents mainly describe street people, criminal and otherwise, although this informal survey found few older words for this label. Today's are all familiar, and include "bums," "substance abusers" (including the earlier "dissolute" and "debauched"), "gang members," "muggers," "beggars," and "panhandlers"—although some of these also double as descriptive terms. In the 1980s, "babies having babies" became popular, and in the 1990s, "illegitimacy" was revived to call particular attention to the poor single-parent family.

Two further types of labels deserve separate attention. The mobile or transient poor have been considered delinquent since at least medieval times, on the assumption that, being mobile, they were free from local social control, and thus expected to turn to crime, mostly economic but also sexual and political, during their wanderings. The list includes "vagabonds," "vagrants," "bums" once more, "street urchins" or "street arabs," "tramps," "shiftless," "lodgers," "hobos," "drifters," "loiterers," and, more recently, "the homeless."

The mobile poor were particularly threatening in the centuries before the invention of the police, and most European languages include labels for them. The other label type might be called class failures, for some labels, including a few already listed above, treat the undeserving poor as being below, or having fallen out of, the class structure. Among these are "residue," "residuum," "dregs," and "lower-lower class"; but the label that banishes the poor from the class hierarchy most literally is "the underclass."

Katz (2013) focuses attention on these "underserving poor." By dividing this group further into drug or alcohol-addicted men, lazy able-bodied men, unmarried mothers, immigrants of various kinds, they are unable to form into a cohesive political force. Thus they are seen as underserving through the stigma created by the label (Katz 2013; Gans 1995) and are politically powerless (Schneider and Ingram 1997). They are at once stereotyped and divided into equally unattractive categories to present cohesive action, and stripped of their individuality to present agency in the face of opposition to accessing help.

Popular culture has picked up on these differences as well. For instance, the musical *Finian's Rainbow* features a song entitled "When the Idle Poor Become the Idle Rich." The song suggests idleness of the poor is no different than idleness of the rich, and if we swap their clothes, one for the other, we would never know the difference as to who is wealthy and who is poor. The lyrics sarcastically identify the labels that are typically assigned to the poor, regardless of their similar actions to those of the rich (ST Lyrics 2017):

> When a rich man doesn't want to work, he's a bon vivant, yes, he's a bon vivant, But when a poor man doesn't want to work, he's a loafer, he's a lounger, he's a lazy good for nothing, he's a jerk.

The poor, underserving or otherwise, have been seen as caught in a culture of poverty, with a host of pressures conducive to immoral behavior. Katz (2013, 26) summarizes such a view from Banfield, who wrote first of an Italian "underclass" and in 1970 of American poor:

> The lower-class person was also impulsive. "Bodily needs (especially for sex) and his taste for 'action' take precedence over anything else—and certainly over any work routine." With a "feeble attenuated sense of self," suffering from "feelings of self-contempt and inadequacy," he remained "suspicious and hostile, aggressive yet dependent," lacking the ability to maintain a stable relationship with a mate, without attachment to community, neighbors, or friends, and with no interest in voluntary organizations or politics. Because the women in the characteristically female-headed lower-class households were usually impulsive and incompetent, boys drifted into gangs where they learned the "extraordinarily violent" style of lower-class life. Lower-class life, in fact, was not normal, and lower-class people emerged from Banfield's account as less than fully human. "In the chapters that follow, the terms *normal* will be used to refer to class culture that is not lower class."

Ravallion (2013, 8) describes these labels over time:

> A long-standing theme in thinking about poverty (still heard today) is that poor people are the cause of the their own poverty. Moral weaknesses are often identified: high fertility, laziness, or bad spending choices; excessive consumption of alcohol was widely identified as a cause of poverty in Europe and North America during the 18th and 19th centuries . . . In more recent times—starting in the late 19th century but not carrying much policy weight

until the second half of the 20th century—deeper causal understanding of poverty pointed to a new role for public action in fighting, and eventually eliminating, persistent poverty.

This new role is made complicated by the actual and perceived extent to which the poor are not fully included in society, by choice or through the legal or social actions taken towards them by those who are not poor. This is the case in suburban settings, where there is a felt desire to "keep up with the Jonses" and not reveal poverty hidden behind the manicured lawns and front porches (Allard 2017; Bryer 2012; Kneebone and Berube 2013); it is the case in rural settings, where residents will drive great distances to use non-cash food assistance (i.e., food stamps) at a market where their neighbors cannot see them (Sherman, 2009); it is the case in urban settings, where underground economies are fully outside normal or legal market systems (Venkatesh 2006).

Perceptions and Included-Out Citizenship

Societies around the world are splintered. The "other" is anyone who looks, speaks, worships, has marital or sexual relations with, eats, or otherwise behaves differently than "I" do. Fear of the "other" is grounded in concern for economic security, preservation of culture or language, preference for status quo living rather than forced change due to demographic shifts, and so on. This fear is reflected in the comment of the woman interviewed in the PBS Frontline episode previously discussed: "I am definitely not a racist. I am not a bigot. I think I hold a little bit of a stigma against people who are different. We don't want nomads who have no roots. I don't want this to be what our community is about."

Erni (2016) describes "others" from a citizenship perspective as those who are "included-out." This means that they are physically taking space in a community, but their status is such as to "insinuate exclusion in the promise of inclusion, or to allow for inclusion in the threat of exclusion" (2016, 331). Cacho (2012) borrows from Espiritu (2003) and describes a similar concept of "differential inclusion." She summarizes: "Certain vulnerable and impoverished populations and places of color have been differentially included within the U.S. legal system. As targets of regulation and containment, they are deemed deserving of discipline and punishment but not worthy of protection. They are not merely excluded from legal protection but criminalized as always already the object and target of law, never its authors or addressees" (Cacho 2012, 5). Marginalized individuals, which include the poor labeled in such ways as we reviewed, are "deemed integral to the nation's economy, culture, identity, and power—but integral only or precisely because of the designated subordinate standing" (Espiritu 2003, 47).

Included-out or differentially included individuals are not necessarily granted the same legal protections as legally recognized citizens but must abide by all laws and regulations, at the risk of being removed from the community through physical, emotional, or cognitive isolation. They may be encouraged to participate politically, but such participation may be observed with skepticism both by authorities and Banfield's "normal" citizens. Likewise, they may be encouraged to express their cultural or religious traditions, or they may be discouraged from doing so.

Implied in the previous paragraph are at least three forms of "citizenship." Building on the work of Cooper (1991; Flathman 1981; Lowi 1981), who differentiated legal from ethical citizenship, we distinguish three forms: legal, political and ethical, and cultural and religious. Figure 2.2 summarizes these distinctions and further differentiates between the "included-out" citizen and its opposite, the "included-in" citizen. The implication is that an individual need not be a legally recognized citizen of a country in order to develop behavioral norms within the cultural or religious fabric, or to seek to enhance quality of life within the cities and communities that they live.

To further this argument that legal citizenship status is not necessary to be an active and/or culturally included citizen, we can visualize the distinction between the included-in and included-out citizen not as fixed cells with

	Legal Citizenship	Political and Ethical Citizenship	Cultural and Religious Citizenship
Included-In	Individual covered by all legal protections with obligation to abide by all laws and regulations	Individual encouraged to participate in candidate and issue advocacy, volunteer, and to vote, insofar as such activity is supported by authorities	Individual free to participate in accepted cultural and religious expression
Included-Out[1]	Individual covered by specifically enumerated legal protections with obligation to abide by all laws and regulations	Individual encouraged to participate, except to vote, insofar as such participation is supported by authorities, and with potential monitoring by authorities	Individual free to participate in accepted cultural and religious expression, with potential limitation and monitoring by authorities

[1] "to insinuate exclusion in the promise of inclusion, or to allow for inclusion in the threat of exclusion" (Erni 2016, 331)

Figure 2.2. Differentiating Forms of Citizenship and Types of Citizens

immovable walls but as open circles with different shades of inclusiveness. The fully included citizen is at the intersection of the three circles, displayed in figure 2.3; the included-out citizens are at the outside perimeter of each circle, the distance between them further symbolizing the negotiation that must be undertaken to understand their unique place in their community. Outside each circle are the fully excluded citizens, who exist physically in shared space but are either not seen, not recognized, or both. These may be illegal immigrants who need, by design, to remain undetected by authorities, or migrants who are continually moving.

Migrants are often economic migrants across countries or within countries. Early poor assistance policies in England and the United States focused on settlement concerns, in which local governments and communities provided support to citizens who were full members of that community—not drifters, Roma, paupers, or others who entered a community not their own in search of work or other support (Katz 1996, 2013), not included-out. We see similar included-out status for ethnic minorities in various countries, with differential status legally, politically, and culturally (Ozolina 2016).

The poor can be considered as included-out or differentially included across all three categories of citizenship activity: legal, political, and ethical, and cultural and religious. Poor legal citizens can vote (unless, in some states,

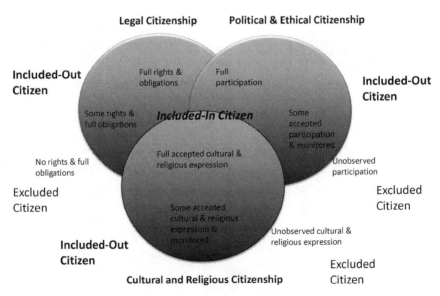

Figure 2.3. Depicting Elastic Boundaries Between Citizens

they have been convicted of a crime), are subject to serving on juries, and must abide by all laws that all legal citizens must abide by: tax law, traffic law, criminal law, civil law. The poor are also often subject to other laws and regulations that do not afford them the same rights as the non-poor. For instance, in some states within the United States, the poor who receive certain public benefits are subject to random drug testing (Cacho 2012). They must report how their public benefit money is spent, how they are searching for employment, and what are their living arrangements. These are intrusions into a legally "sacred" idea embedded in much of American culture: privacy.

Once imprisoned for committing a crime, a person loses more rights and is subject to more control over their persons and behaviors. The materially poor are more likely to be imprisoned than those who are more well off and thus differentially included or included-out as a legal matter, as well as in status. In sum, research indicates that materially poor are more likely to commit crime, more likely to be convicted of said crime, more likely to remain poor after being reintroduced to society once they have served their time, and their family left "behind" while the person who was in prison is likely to remain in poverty. The cycle of material poverty is pretty firm in this context. The poor are more likely to be included-out than the non-poor.

In the state of Florida, for example, the plight of felons, most of whom come from impoverished backgrounds, is exemplified by a headline from the *Miami Herald*: Thousands of Florida felons wait decades to regain the right to vote (Bousquet 2017). In Florida, the right of a convicted felon to vote, own a gun, or run for office is permanently revoked, subject to appeal. This system has disenfranchised approximately 1.5 million people; after they serve their time, they must wait an additional five years before being eligible to apply for restoration of rights. Currently, the Board of Executive Clemency considers only 400 cases per year with nearly 20,000 eligible for consideration (Bousquet 2017). This is a clear example of a population that is specifically included-out, which specifically has, by virtue of the people who commit most crimes, affected the lives of the poor.

Impoverished individuals are not, as a general scientific principle, more likely to commit crime due to a different psychological wiring in the brain; crime is committed as a strategy of survival. Jean Val Jean in *Les Misérables* steals a loaf of bread to feed himself, is caught, and is thus subjected to a lifetime of hardship. He does not get the job he seeks after release from prison because he is an ex-prisoner. His status poverty is high. His opportunity for life transformation comes only after he steals again to survive but is set free, not because the criminal justice system was forgiving but because the victim of the crime perceived what amounted to legitimate theft.

As a society, the idea of "legitimate theft" is not legally nor generally morally recognized. In other words, theft in order to survive is punishable to the same extent as theft committed for greed, malice, or for fun. Impoverished individuals are subject to the same criminal laws as non-poor people, but they are legally restricted in other ways, given their lost privacy as they collect public benefits for housing, food, job training, et cetera. They are legally included-out; they are marginalized (Cacho 2012).

This idea of "legitimate theft" is the subject of an interesting ethical and philosophical text (Mancilla 2016). Are there any conditions under which an individual has a right to take, or to steal, something that is legally the property of another? Does a human being have a "right of necessity" to break the law for the purpose of survival? This can include the hungry person who steals some food from the local market, or the homeless person who escapes the cold or heat by breaking and entering into someone's property for shelter. There are "rules" established by Mancilla (2016, 4) that can guide, from an ethical perspective, what is proper. These include:

- "The need is basic"
- "The person in need does not violate other equally important moral interests to exercise her right"
- "It is a last resort"

Laws are not always derived based on ethics but tend to be blunt instruments that conceive of the world in black and white terms. The law is broken, or it is not broken. Poverty contributes to the need to break the law, even if doing so is (arguably) ethically defensible. The need for breaking the law, and the subsequent act of breaking it, further set poor people apart from the non-poor, and chronic deprivation both relegates the poor to included-out status and pushes the poor towards behaviors that are potentially less legally and socially acceptable in the interest of survival.

Another example of this is in the area of child welfare. Stephanie Clifford and Jessica Silver-Greenberg write in the *New York Times* about a series of women whose behavior with their children is criminalized despite, though perhaps not strictly wise and safe, not constituting neglect. Yet they are behaviors of necessity as women who are poor and who lack full support for child rearing. One such woman is Maisa Joefield (Clifford and Silver-Greenberg 2017, MB1):

Maisha Joefield thought she was getting by pretty well as a young single mother in Brooklyn, splurging on her daughter, Deja, even though money was tight. When Deja was a baby, she bought her Luvs instead of generic diapers when she could. When her daughter got a little older, Ms. Joefield outfitted the bedroom in their apartment with a princess bed for Deja, while she slept on a pullout couch.

She had family around, too. Though she had broken up with Deja's father, they spent holidays and vacations together for Deja's sake. Ms. Joefield's grandmother lived across the street, and Deja knew she could always go to her great-grandmother's apartment in an emergency.

One night, exhausted, Ms. Joefield put Deja to bed, and plopped into a bath with her headphones on.

"By the time I come out, I'm looking, I don't see my child," said Ms. Joefield, who began frantically searching the building. Deja, who was 5, had indeed headed for the grandmother's house when she couldn't find her mother, but the next thing Ms. Joefield knew, it was a police matter.

"I'm thinking, I'll explain to them what happened, and I'll get my child," Ms. Joefield said.

For most parents, this scenario might be a panic-inducing, but hardly insurmountable, hiccup in the long trial of raising a child. Yet for Ms. Joefield and women in her circumstances—living in poor neighborhoods, with few child care options—the consequences can be severe. Police officers removed Deja from her apartment and the Administration for Children's Services placed her in foster care. Police charged Ms. Joefield with endangering the welfare of a child.

It is not only in legal terms that the poor are included-out. Previously, we suggested that the greater likelihood of the poor to commit crime is not a consequence of different psychological "wiring." As a matter of criminal psychology, this is true; however, those who grow up in poverty do in fact grow up to be wired differently. The psychology of the poor is different than that of the non-poor. The behavioral consequence of these differences increases status poverty as well as agency poverty.

Jensen (2009) identifies four risk factors that shape cognitive development of children, which affects academic and social performance, which in turn affects prospects for employment and relationships in adulthood. These factors are: emotional and social challenges, acute and chronic stressors, cognitive lags, and health and safety issues.

"Typically," writes Jensen (2009, 15), "the weak or anxious attachments formed by infants in poverty become the basis for full-blown insecurity during the early childhood years." Citing a host of social-psychological research, Jensen observes that parent-child relationships and attachments form the basis for future relationships and development of core social functions, including arousal, emotional regulation, independence, and social competence (Szewcyk-Sokolowski, Bost, and Wainwright 2005; Sroufe 2005). To develop these social functions, children require caregivers who provide consistent love and support, demonstrated reciprocal interactions, and engagement in increasingly complex environments. Children raised in poverty are likely to be denied exposure to these needed interactions. Jensen (2009, 16) summarizes: "Deficits in these areas inhibit the production of new brain cells, alter the path of maturation, and rework healthy neural circuitry in children's brains, thereby undermining emotional and social development and predisposing them to emotional dysfunction" (Gunnar, Frenn, Wewerka, and Van Ryzin 2009; Miller, Seifer, Stroud, Sheinkopf, and Dickstein 2006).

When poor children act in a manner inconsistent with social norms, their teachers and other adults representing "middle class" values may treat them as delinquent or mischievous rather than as not "properly" developed. The punishments, low academic marks, or other consequences of behavior that is not normal push the child into a self-fulfilling and vicious cycle of failure and further increases in status and agency poverty. The more the poor, developing child is treated according to norms of "typical" behaviors and not appropriately to his or her cognitive, social, and emotional development, the more likely they will come to see the "achievement ideology" embedded within American culture (e.g., if I work hard, I will succeed) as not applying to them (MacLeod 2009).

The second risk factor is acute and chronic stressors. Poor children are more likely to experience acute stress, which is "severe stress resulting from exposure to such trauma as abuse or violence," and chronic stress, which is "high stress sustained over time" (Jensen 2009, 22). This kind of stress negatively affects brain functioning and capacity to develop coping skills, resulting in behavioral and academic problems. Jensen (2009, 24) summarizes the unique stressors in the lives of the poor:

> The frequency and intensity of both stressful life events and daily hassles are greater among low-SES children (Attar, Guerra, and Tolan, 1994). For example, in any given year, more than half of all poor children deal with evic-

tions, utility disconnections, overcrowding, or lack of a stove or refrigerator, compared with only 13 percent of well-off children (Lichter 1997). In addition, such factors as lack of proper supervision, physical neglect or abuse, inadequate day care and schools, difficulties in forming healthy friendships, and vulnerability to depression combine to exert inordinate and debilitating stress upon the developing child.

In sum, the stressors associated with the impoverished life are both physiologically and psychologically disruptive and sources of stress, which piles on in the form of social exclusion. Poverty begets stressful situations that beget gaps in academic achievement and socialization within community, which beget exclusion, thus adding to the stressors.

Exclusionary forces are also keyed into the lack of communication skills, which are grounded in poverty. As Jensen (2009, 35) explains: "By the time most children start school, they will have been exposed to 5 million words and should know about 13,000 of them. By high school, they should know about 60,000 to 100,000 words (Huttenlocher 1998). But that doesn't often happen in low-income homes. Weizman and Snow (2001) found that low-income caregivers speak in shorter, more grammatically simple sentences. There is less back-and-forth—fewer questions asked and fewer explanations given. As a result, children raised in poverty experience a more limited range of language capabilities."

David Brooks (2017, A23), columnist for the *New York Times* writes about an experience he had with someone with less education than he that makes this point.

> Recently I took a friend with only a high school degree to lunch. Insensitively, I led her into a gourmet sandwich shop. Suddenly I saw her face freeze up as she was confronted with sandwiches named "Padrino" and "Pomodoro" and ingredients like soppressata, capicollo and a striata baguette. I quickly asked her if she wanted to go somewhere else and she anxiously nodded yes and we ate Mexican.

> American upper-middle-class culture (where the opportunities are) is now laced with cultural signifiers that are completely illegible unless you happen to have grown up in this class. They play on the normal human fear of humiliation and exclusion. Their chief message is, "You are not welcome here."

All of this contributes to status poverty and the idea of being included-out or differentially included, legally, politically, and ethically, and culturally and religiously. The failure to "fit in" fully makes the poor not credible participants in political dialogue or other forms of participation, potentially less welcomed as volunteers within the broader community, and less able to share with a broader non-poor population unique attributes of their cultural life. They are excluded from "normal" culture (Currid-Halkett 2017) and cannot easily invite "normal" into their culture.

With a presentation of the individual subjective and societal inter-subjective realities laid plane, we turn to the statistics on subsistence and agency poverty.

Objective Measures of Poverty

Poverty is multi-dimensional and multi-faceted. As observed is the subjective and societal inter-subjective perceptions of poverty and the poor, the issue is not only about money, housing, clothing, or other material goods. It is about actual and perceived power, actual and perceived access to services, and actual and perceived access to opportunities. These multiple dimensions are reflected in measures of subsistence and agency poverty; status poverty is reflected in the inter-subjective perceptions previously discussed.

Subsistence Poverty

The 2016 poverty thresholds in the United States are defined by income based on a formula initially developed and deployed in 1963. Specifically, the threshold is the income required to maintain a basic diet, calculated to be one third of a family budget, multiplied by three to cover all other basic life costs. The threshold is used to report official poverty statistics within the country; a separate measure called the poverty guideline is used for determining eligibility for various government programs. Guidelines use the poverty threshold as a base but adjust to include various other supplemental costs as well as possibly adjustments for cost of living across different geographies (Fisher 1992).

Since the War on Poverty was launched in 1964, with the passage of the Economic Opportunity Act, poverty rates have remained high, insofar as poverty has not been eradicated. Opponents of government entitlement and assistance programs consider the same basic rates of poverty to be a sign that such government investments to support the needy are not effective in actually reducing either the incidence of poverty or overall poverty rates. Advocates of such programs suggest without the programs, those who are materially poor would exist in a much poorer condition, and, though the overall poverty rate might be reduced, individual impoverished people are helped through the programs.

As of 2012, 46 million Americans were living in poverty, including 16 million children (Lewis and Alexander 2015). Most families who are in poverty are short-term or temporarily impoverished, one year or less. Twelve percent are in poverty for at least ten years (Iceland 2012). According to the Census Bureau, in 2011, 16 percent of Americans are poor, 22 percent of children are in poverty (37 percent of black children and 34 percent of Hispanic children). Forty-eight percent of female-headed households are in poverty, compared to 11 percent of households with married couples.

Ten to 12 percent of Americans have an income below 50 percent of the poverty threshold, including 7 percent of children. This is an income level that is considered as "deep poverty," and the rate has remained basically stable over the past fifty years, an "intransigence" that "is surprising" (Fox, Wimer, Garfinkel, Kaushal, Nam, and Waldfogel 2015, 14). Without cash and non-cash assistance programs, Fox et al. (2015) estimate that deep poverty would have increased from 12.8 to 18.7 percent between 1968 and 2011. In this period, families without an employed adult are much more likely today to be in deep poverty; single parent families are less likely to be in deep poverty, and households without children are more likely to be in deep poverty compared to households with children (Fox et al. 2015).

Ron Haskins (2014, 5) summarizes the state of poverty over the past fifty years after enactment of War on Poverty programs:

- Government spending on poor and low-income families has increased almost every year for five decades; since 1980 spending has tripled as measured on a per person in poverty basis in constant dollars;
- An improved measure of poverty shows that government spending focused on poor and low-income households cuts the poverty rate by about half; government spending on these programs and the Unemployment Compensation program prevented poverty from increasing during the most severe recession since the Great Depression;
- A CBO analysis shows that when government benefits are counted at their full value, households all along the income distribution, including those in the bottom 20 percent, enjoyed increased income between 1979 and 2007;
- The same CBO report shows that because income increased more the higher up we look in the income distribution between 1979 and 2007, income inequality has also increased since 1979; by far the biggest increase in inequality is between the top and the rest of the distribution;
- Several studies show that claims that intergenerational income mobility has slowed down in the United States are false; the United States

has less income mobility than many European nations, but mobility has remained constant over the past four decades or so; nonetheless, children whose parents were in the bottom 20 percent of the income distribution have more than a 40 percent chance of staying in the bottom themselves.

Barriers to mobility out of poverty are multiple, including family instability and insecurity, access to labor markets for unskilled workers, and public policies that fail to address root issues such as family formation, family resources, health, education, and neighborhoods (Smeeding 2016). Family instability and insecurity is characterized by what Smeeding (2016, 99) calls the "parenting gap" and "diverging destinies." Children in families with more financially secure parents are provided more opportunities for life exploration and advancement, including access to better education, culture, travel, and family togetherness (Brooks 2017; Currid-Halkett 2017; Reeves 2017). With respect to labor markets, low-skilled factory jobs that used to provide access to middle class lifestyles are all but disappeared, particularly with automation of more activities; advanced training is necessary to gain access to employment that is well paid.

Thanks in large measure to increasingly generous social security benefits first introduced during the Franklin Delano Roosevelt administration and other cash and non-cash assistance programs, poverty rates among the elderly have been well managed. Haskins (2014, 1) summarizes: "[P]overty among the elderly fell to 25 percent in 1968 from 35 percent in 1950, a reduction of almost 30 percent during the Johnson Presidency. Elderly poverty continued to fall after 1968. In 2012, a year in which the overall poverty rate was 15 percent and the child poverty rate nearly 22 percent, the poverty rate among the elderly was about 9 percent."

Overall, with respect to subsistence poverty, the record over the past fifty years is mixed; some statistics remain stubbornly high, though they might have been worse in the absence of certain assistance programs. We can suggest poverty is being fought, with individual battles being won with certain demographics, but the full war is ongoing.

Agency Poverty

As an extended metaphor, let us consider the story by Ursula Le Guin, "The Ones Who Walk Away from Omelas." In a fictional town with the name Omelas, Le Guin tells us about a place that is beautiful and a people who enjoy a positive, no-stress existence. The weather is perfect; there is no drug use; there is no crime; animals are well behaved; children infect each other with laughter; men and women are free, open, and supportive of each other. The world as it exists in Omelas is perfect, except for one thing.

Hidden within a closet or a deep cellar somewhere within Omelas is a child, naked, and malnourished. The child is not permitted any human contact, exposure to the beautiful sunshine, to see the outside world, listen to the music or enjoy the laughter. Occasionally a citizen from Omelas will enter the cellar, throw food at the child, kick it, and torment it. The rule in Omelas is that for the beauty and happiness to exist outside, the child must remain in this deprived situation.

Let us pause from Le Guin's story to reflect on its meaning for combatting poverty. In the story, a citizen who is included-out, the child in the cellar, is forgotten by the masses. The rest in the community are operating based on an ethical assumption of utilitarianism—the greatest good for the greatest number. The poor, represented by the child, must endure extreme hardship without a voice and without power to affect change. This is reflective of the impoverishment experienced by many: it is out of site, or hidden in plain view. It is not engaged, and a willingness to address it is limited by a popular understanding of what "it" is.

Returning to Omelas, Le Guin tells us how the people of the city were aware of the suffering of the child. One by one, without consulting their friends or neighbors, they quietly walked away, leaving the city, the beauty, and the ever-present but not always visible dark cloud of the suffering, impoverished child.

These are the included-in citizens and do in fact reflect individuals populating cities throughout the United States and much of the world. Those who have the potential to engage, who are socially accepted, economically self-sufficient, and generally socially aware are determining to not engage as citizens. This is impoverished citizenship that is not related to subsistence poverty; citizens are fully included-in but choose to exist from the outside. They are included-out by choice, leaving a sub-elite to exert disproportionate amounts of influence in policymaking. The state of civics for the included-out by choice is summarized (Bryer 2014, 16):

> [A]s citizens, in our collective ignorance and mutual distrust, we tend to follow each other, thus creating the equivalent of lemmings running off a cliff en masse because no one knew enough to think or act differently than the popular opinion of the moment indicated. Those who do not follow may disengage in the face of what they perceive to be an uphill battle against the mass, and if they did engage, the mass may likely not trust them enough to change course.

To suggest the fault of non-participation rests solely with the choice of included-in citizens is not entirely accurate. Institutions of government, media, academia, and faith organizations erect plentiful barriers to participation. These barriers prevent empowerment of those who should, by social acceptance, culture, and economics, have all capability to engage meaningfully, to represent self, and to seek to engage, empower, and represent others. As Bryer (2014, 17) writes, continuing the summary: "Adding to this quagmire of collective ignorance and mutual distrust are the very real mechanisms, institutions, and procedures in place that actively 'demobilize citizens' (Crenson and Ginsberg 2002). These procedures include the extent that money pervades the political process (Broder 2000), the pre-scripted feel of public hearings (Baker, Addams, and Davis 2005), the special interest-dominated policymaking process (Casper 2000), and the generally inaccessible government documents that call for public comments" (Bryer 2013).

On the occasion of government asking these otherwise privileged citizens to participate, there are barriers that dissuade the potentially active citizen. In such scenarios, they. . . . "May often find that they have insufficient information, guidance, and/or confidence to do so effectively, leading to further disempowerment, demobilization, distrust, and further restricted opportunities for meaningful engagement" (Bryer 2014, 17).

In other words, included-in is not a steady-state status; it is changeable, dependent on individual initiative and institutional capacity and inducement. The state of impoverished citizenship for those who are not materially poor is high; agency poverty is high for a subset of the privileged included-in class.

This contrasts with the subsistence poor who are included-out based on legal requirement, social expectation, or cultural norm. Desire to be involved, to self-present, is thwarted not only by institutional barriers of the kind that plague the privileged included-in; desire is thwarted by the high levels of status poverty and agency poverty discussed previously. What we have then are blurred boundaries; the materially poor and non-materially poor are equally poor in measures of citizenship.

International Dimensions of Poverty

The United States is unique in how it treats poverty and in the kinds of poverty experienced by citizens. Two main conclusions in the global comparison: (1) The United States has the highest proportion of workers in relatively poorly paid jobs, and (2) the United States has relatively lower spending on social programs and support. Both of these combined contribute to the United States having one of the highest rates of poverty in the world.

Simply stated, the combination of low pay and low social spending reinforce each other, rather than counteract each other.

Burtless and Smeeding (2007, 7) summarize the United States case in comparison to other nations:

> The lowest poverty rates are more common in smaller, well-developed, and high-spending welfare states (Sweden, Finland) where they are about 5 or 6 percent. Middle level rates are found in major European countries where social policies provide more generous support to single mothers and working women (through paid family leave, for example), and where social assistance minimums are high. For instance, the Netherlands, Austria, Belgium, and Germany have poverty rates that are in the 8 to 9 percent range, while France is at 7 percent. Even the former Soviet block nations of Estonia, Poland, and Slovenia, and Taiwan, have much lower poverty rates than does the United States.

As we will see in the chapters that follow, the philosophy of treating poverty and lifting people out of poverty is unique in the Unites States, thus enabling these gaps between nations. As we consider new solutions to poverty in all its forms, we will look to examples from outside the United States for inspiration and to test the applicability of ideas within these other contexts.

Summary

Pimpare (2017) closes his essay by asking some questions, somewhat rhetorical but all demanding an answer: "Why do we begrudge people struggling to get by the occasional indulgence? Why do we so little value pleasure and joy? Why do we insist that if you are poor, you should also be miserable? Why do we require penitence?" In this chapter, we considered the meaning of "us" or the poor. Pimpare is challenging not "us" but "we"—those who are not poor, who have means, status, and agency. "We" are considered in the next chapter, in the context of discussing "with."

Note

1. See http://www.povertysimulation.org

CHAPTER THREE

~

With or Without Us

In this chapter, we focus on the other component of the slogan, "Nothing about us without us is for us." Specifically, what does it mean for policymaking and implementation to be "without" us or the opposite "with" us? Here we will spend much more time analyzing the meanings of Maximum Feasible Participation, as it was developed in the 1960s United States and how it is still interpreted today. Referring to the concept map (figure 1.1), whereas chapter 2 contains explication of the kinds of poverty, in this chapter we emphasize forms of citizenship as a means to distinguish inclusion from exclusion in society.

Melish (2010) makes a set of assumptions regarding the unique ability of individuals, with lived experience, to represent their own best interests. For instance, she writes, "How to create a new set of era-appropriate national orchestration mechanisms and policy arrangements through which the voices and constructive input of *the poor—those best situated to identify day-to-day barriers to opportunity*—can continually be taken into account by the regulatory apparatus in practical social-welfare policymaking" (2010, 11, italics added).

In describing Maximum Feasible Participation she writes: "The concept was simple: those most affected by social disadvantage . . . were *necessarily better positioned to understand poverty's causes, to identify the most effective solutions to them, and to advocate their own communities' interests* than were 'outside' middle-class professional reformers lacking any direct experience with those conditions" (Melish 2010, 18, italics added). Such participation of the poor, she suggests, "would ensure that programs were in fact responding flexibly to changing community needs and priorities, being communicated in effective and culturally appropriate ways, and leading to actual measurable improvements in the lived realities of impoverished communities" (2010, 18).

This is a logic that concerns not just poverty but spans social and economic issues and groups of all kinds. A recent report concerning juvenile justice included a central recommendation that any reform to the system must include juveniles as active participants (Pittsburgh Foundation 2017); women's activist groups regularly charge male-dominated legislative bodies as acting illegitimately when making policy decisions that affect women's health, for instance, without any women present; students are regularly granted participation on university governing boards, and so on.

This intuitively appealing idea, that we as individuals best know our lives and the issues that affect our lives and are thus best able to represent our interests on matters that will help or harm us, is anathema to the logic presented by the founding thinkers of the United States. James Madison and Alexander Hamilton wrote in their respective *Federalist Papers*—essays written in defense of the newly drafted U.S. Constitution—how the people themselves are incapable of reason, that they are driven by emotion and subject to "temporary delusion" (Bryer and Cooper 2012). In other words, the people themselves are better to entrust decisions that concern them to a more sedate body of representatives who, through their detachment, can dispassionately assess benefits and drawbacks for any citizen or group of citizens.

The fragmentation of the U.S. governmental system is grounded in these assumptions, including even the lower chamber of the House of Representatives intended to be closer to the people and thus more likely subject to unreasonable passion, matched with the upper chamber of the U.S. Senate. The Senate was initially designed as a body not elected through popular vote, creating more distance. Even with the popular election process firmly in place, with terms of six years, Senators are more insulated from the emotional whims of the people—at least this is the argument.

As such, the phrase "nothing about us without us is for us" is really complex, and a counter phrase may just as legitimately be considered, such as: anything about us with us potentially deceives us. Deception is in the form of manipulation and can be interpreted to mean, "us" are used, manipulated, befuddled, and ultimately giving credibility to the decisions made "about us" even if those views are more objectively for some other group. During the summer of 2017, there was a fierce debate in Congress about the repeal and replacement of the Affordable Care Act (also known as Obamacare) Democrats charged Republicans with suggesting the proposed reforms are "for" the working poor but in reality are more beneficial for the rich. The working poor have not been active participants in generating reform proposals, but they were effectively "used" and have given credibility through their vote in the 2016 elections. This "using" is not unique to the current debate on healthcare, and an equal argument might just as easily be made about election and policy politics engaged in by Democratic party leaders as Republican party leaders.

In these pages, we unpack and analyze these competing phrases a bit more, calling on theories of representation, power, and responsiveness. Following this assessment, we consider the meaning of Maximum Feasible Participation and suggest that its implementation has not adhered to the values and assumptions of the first phrase (nothing about us without us is for us), has edged closer to the second phrase (anything about us with us potentially deceives us), and has opened up doors to a third phrase (anything without us . . . makes us adversaries).

Representation

To represent is to stand for, speak for, and/or act for those who either cannot stand, speak, or act for themselves, or who do not have the time or interest to do so. There is a conundrum here, though, on both the side of the represented and the representative.

On the represented side, the idea that someone, the poor specifically, cannot, or do not have the time or interest, in standing, speaking, or acting for themselves, is anathema to Melish's argument. Specifically, she suggests the poor are the best to present their experiences and ideas themselves, not to be filtered by elite, celebrity, or special interest representatives—however well meaning.

However, the powerlessness of the poor, reinforced institutionally, culturally, and socially renders their ability to self-present or to hold a designated representative accountable a distant goal rather than a probable reality. As such, self-appointed representatives "represent" the poor in the halls of power, in city councils and state and national legislatures. These are individuals or organizations that ensure the "voice" of the poor is fully presented in decision-making processes. However, the poor do not consistently have the power to hold these self-appointed representatives to account. As such, the representation provided is not fully democratic but is by proxy. The lack of accountability limits power and places a cap on democratic potential. As such, the challenge is to represent while trying to cultivate power.

We examine the dynamics of power further, but this discussion will benefit from a close look at an example from the implementation of Maximum Feasible Participation principles during the early years of the War on Poverty. Through this example we consider specifically the question: are the poor capable of presenting their own interests? If so, will the non-poor bestow upon them the credibility needed to present their own interests? If not, how can the self-appointed representatives of the poor best be held to account? We consider broadly these questions before introducing the example.

Are the poor capable of presenting their own interests? This is a perplexing question, as first it must be understood what the interests of the poor are. President Donald Trump in June 2017 made a statement that he did not want to employ a poor person as an economic advisor; he preferred extraordinarily wealthy successful businessmen. This is perhaps not a unique position to be held by presidents of either party, but President Trump may be the first to vocalize it in such stark terms. The broader implication of this idea is that those titans of Wall Street, as the case is, know better about financial markets and regulations, thus enabling policies that can strengthen economic performance. Improved performance should lift up the boat to help the poor gain access to jobs and well-paying jobs. In other words, individuals who know how to manipulate policy, legal, and regulatory levers of the economy can best meet the interests of the poor. The poor are not capable of representing more than their lived experience; they are not capable of defining the solutions necessary to solve the problems they encounter.

Recent survey research found that those who are financially struggling are more likely to want stable employment with regular paychecks rather than opportunities to advance and increase their pay rate over time. This preference or interest in stability over growth might not be reflected in policy decisions framed by non-poor representatives. As such, we can suggest the poor can best present their goals and desires and values.

Even this can be challenged as goal achievement might not always align with values-based strategies. For instance, Sherman (2009) describes how some people examined in an enthnographic study of rural poor resisted seeking government support, and if they did, they incurred the cost of driving a long distance to the next town to utilize cash assistance for food so as to avoid the negative perception of their peers. White (2009) and Bryer (2012) describe how those who are poor in suburban areas will not reveal their plight to neighbors or friends for fear of being labeled lazy, shiftless, or irresponsible. MacLeod (2009) reveals how some simply did not make long-term goals as they accepted a destiny of poverty and mere survival.

To not accept that the poor can best present their goals and desires and values, however, is to assign them no agency at all, and in so doing, our institutions are complicit through their lack of investment to educate and empower. When we accept a lack of capacity for self-presentation in the most basic action of coherent self-expression (e.g., stating interests, values, and goals), we declare defeat in any war on poverty that might ensue.

That said, we must recognize that the ability for any individual to make rational, informed decisions, with clear understanding of the relationship between action and consequence, is based at least partially on the ability to manage the number of stimuli in one's environment (Lupia and McCubbins 1998). The more noise or distractions or needs or people around us at any one time challenges one's ability to focus, learn, and act in the most appropriate way. As discussed in the previous chapter, children who grow up in poverty have multiple survival stimuli that need attention, leaving little room for non-survival academic pursuits. This persists into adulthood, meaning even if there was a desire to self-present, to have the time and ability to have a truly distraction-free environment is problematic.

If the answer to our question (Are the poor capable of presenting their own interests?) is "yes," it must be a highly qualified yes. For the ability to achieve equality in procedural democracy, meaning all people including the poor are equally empowered, requires, we suggest, attention to substantive democracy. Distractions, extra stimuli, et cetera, must be mitigated so participation in self-presentation and democratic discourse is no longer a luxury.

That it is a luxury, or can be treated as a luxury, renders the second question to be equally vexing. Will the non-poor bestow upon the poor the credibility needed to present their own interests? If self-presentation and democratic engagement is considered as something to be earned by the elite, any of the masses who mobilize or seek to disrupt are at risk of being labeled as a mob without individual agency nor individual freedom. The mob will act in turn, as individuals will lean on their compatriots as guides for engaging against a political system and policy process that is perceived to be non-responsive.

A mob can be conceived as emotionally driven and not reasonable, exactly how the writers of the Federalist Papers assume the masses to be. As Woodrow Wilson writes, we must suffer the meddlesomeness of the people, of the masses, as the United States is a democracy. However, there is no reasonableness there, and the stereotype of the poor is worse than that— lazy, shiftless, undeserving, et cetera. As discussed in the previous chapter, if individuals are unwilling to have the poor live next door, why would we expect comfort in letting their voice have equal weight as "ours" in public discourse?

Pulling this together then, and reconnecting with previous discussions on the three types of poverty, we can offer this summary assessment: The subsistence poor will have a questionable amount of agency, at best, and if developed or used, their agency will be challenged on account of their perceived status in society. Melish's passionately written passages suggesting that the poor are the best to represent themselves and thus should be engaged through a 21st century Maximum Feasible Participation, ultimately fall flat. Without empowerment in the form of belief in agency and enhanced status, free from manipulation, self-presentation will not be achieved, and the interests best presented by the poor themselves will not be fully understood nor properly acted upon.

The poor will be reliant in this scenario on self-appointed representatives, the compassion of empathetic non-poor individuals, or some combination of both. Empathy or the capacity to show empathy, however, might not be a noble trait. As Bloom (2016) suggests, empathy is akin to a sugary soda: it might taste good, and our ability to show it might make us and individuals around us feel good, but it is as a regular part of daily life a negative, irrational reaction.

First, we must consider, what is the empathy of a self-appointed representative? What is the empathy of someone like Bono from the band, U2, for the global poor? What is the empathy of special interest group representatives who lobby government officials for policy change, or organize the poor themselves to aggressively demand new services and benefits?

Without naming it as such, Dina Leygerman criticized the idea and practice of empathy (2017):

> I don't know what it's like to try to make ends meet by having to work multiple low paying jobs, or what it's like to raise a child without a spouse, or what it's like to live in a community where hopelessness is rampant. I don't know what it's like to attend a school with no supplies, where crime is prevalent, where teachers are hardly paid, where most children have not eaten in the morning or even the day(s) before. I don't know what it's like to be born into a world where your toilet is an outhouse, where you stand in line at a soup kitchen, where you rely on charity for your basic needs. I don't know what it's like to spend winters without heat, summers without air conditioning, every day without clean water. I don't know what it's like to live to survive, to not know when my next meal will come, to make impossible decision every day. I don't know what it's like to be poor. I am privileged.

And yet so many of us pretend we know. Can't they just go get a job? Can't they just work harder? Can't they just go get a degree? Can't they just save more? Spend less? These questions are ridiculous. They come from people who have never known any struggles. They come from people who never held multiple jobs just to put food on the table. These questions are from people who assume hard work is the answer to all problems. These questions are from people who were not born into poverty.

In this passage she is mostly critiquing those who promote policies that are "harsh" in setting limits, timelines, resource constraints, drug tests, et cetera on the poor. This is not so much an issue of empathy; for those who preach such policy prescriptions, we can suggest there is a decided lack of empathy, a lack of imagining oneself "walking in the shoes" of the poor. Read another way, Leygerman's statement is an indictment of empathy entirely. For those who actually do not nor ever have walked in the shoes of the poor, to prescribe increases in food support, enhancement of job training programs, or provision of educational grants—however intuitively appealing—is as potentially damaging to the actual physical, emotional, or material condition of the poor as the application of strict work requirements, drug testing mandates, and food support limitation.

This is Bloom's (2016) essential argument. Acting on behalf of another or a whole group of people thinking that we know them and what life experiences they have endured—a cognitive empathy—is likely to lead to manipulation or attempted manipulation. Say the right thing without connecting emotionally. To achieve an emotional connection is fleeting and potentially drives those who have good intention to act irrationally.

Melish (2010) provides an example that identifies the drawbacks of self-appointed representatives and empathetic others as deployed in the early years of the War on Poverty. She observes that outsiders to the communities entered with the intent to mobilize the poor, to demand resources and services guaranteed through War on Poverty legislation, and essentially push the capacity of local governments to the breaking point. Such a strategy enabled these outsiders to effectively lobby for more resources, protections for the poor, social service programs, and financial well-being packages.

Maximum Feasible Participation of the poor became, in this implementation, maximum feasible manipulation of the poor. The outsiders, elites by all standards (e.g., education, wealth, life privileges), were acting on behalf of the poor, representing the poor, but failing to enable or empower the poor to represent themselves or to hold their self-appointed representatives to account (Montanaro 2012). The drive for being a self-appointed representative may have been based on a lust for power, or it may have been based on a true empathetic concern. Acting on that empathy led to policies that not only failed to empower the poor, they made clear divisions that exist between the poor and non-poor, between the privileged and strained, and between the powerful and powerless.

Ultimately, to achieve effective, accountable representation of the poor by the non-poor, or to allow the poor to self-present their own interests, requires genuine empowerment. This is the lesson from the Maximum Feasible Participation of the War on Poverty. Outsiders who enter a community, with good intention, who manipulate the masses without ensuring sustainable empowerment of the poor and who generate empathy-based temporary support for the poor, will see power deteriorate and public support erode.

Power

Sherry Arnstein (1969) conceptualized power between government and citizens as a "zero sum" situation. The amount of power in a society, community, et cetera, is finite. As such, when one group gives power away, another group becomes more powerful; the authority of giving or taking power rests with the government as an institution. To demonstrate these dynamics, Arnstein presents a ladder of participation, at the bottom of which are two forms of non-participation where citizens do not have any power. Each rung of the ladder upward assumes citizens are given more and more power, until the top when they exercise full control.

The mass of citizens does not exist as one on Arnstein's ladder. Some citizens are more powerful than others, given their money, networks, and influence. The poor are weak. They have limited means to engage in political theatre; they have limited networks that can be leveraged to promote policy agendas; they are relatively disconnected agents and, given their "station in life" are not granted opportunity to engage meaningfully. This lack of power, occupying the bottom rungs of the ladder, is confounded by the lack of a single group within the impoverished population. Some, to use Schneider and Ingram's (1997) language, are deserving of care and attention from political elites; others are undeserving. The deserving are dependent on the state and the goodwill of others, and generally they will receive support in a generally passive way; the undeserving are deviants and are not likely to gain access to the resources they need to manage, let alone escape, their impoverished situation. The impact is a structural inequality built into the political culture and institutional arrangements intended to engage communities in a war on poverty.

Whether dependents or deviants, the poor are subject to manipulation and therapy and information sharing: limited power, and, perhaps most damaging, the appearance of empowerment only. Indeed, there is a potentially fine line between these bottom rungs and empowerment, or more precisely between manipulation and empowerment, as seen in figure 3.1.

The ease of manipulation to occur with the poor, or any population, has in the past turned the most idealistic democrats into cautious republicans who have been chastened by what they perceive as some combination of apathy, ignorance, and manipulation of the masses (Fink 1997). In other words, the masses cannot be empowered, as they are ignorant and perhaps do not care about their ignorance, or do not have time to correct for their ignorance. As such, they cannot present their own views; they cannot be effective advocates for their own causes, as Melish (2010) argues they alone can best be. This is a potentially psychological barrier to empowerment.

This kind of psychological barrier, or perceived barrier, is something that U.S. Housing and Urban Development Secretary Ben Carson was criticized for in remarks made in spring 2017 (Alcindor 2017). He suggested that poverty is a "state of mind." His point was that an individual with a strong work ethic and will to achieve can overcome whatever constraints are placed

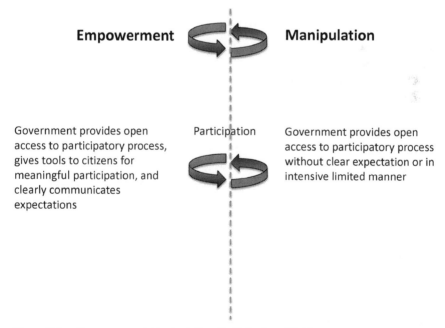

Figure 3.1. Empowerment-Manipulation Participatory Divide

upon him or her by the binds of poverty. We will return to this idea in a later chapter, but we can apply the same logic, perhaps more successfully, to the idea of empowerment.

Empowerment is a state of mind. If a person feels powerful, they will be able to reach beyond their self- or other-imposed constraints and achieve what or succeed in ways they did not think possible.

There is a problem with states of mind, though. They tend to not be fixed and can be manipulated. They are malleable. The *feeling* of empowerment is not the same as *actual* empowerment. We can create institutions and systems that allow the poor to have seats at the proverbial table, but unless those seats are more numerous than tokenistic and constructed to be the same height as all other seats, then the empowerment is false and symbolic. They are power and participation that are fake (Snyder 2011).

This indeed is the conundrum: how to empower when empowerment, if it is possible, requires manipulation? Stated differently: Is it possible to empower without manipulation when the masses, poor or otherwise, are ignorant, powerless, and blissfully so? Is it possible to empower when the powerless do not seek and do not accept the power offered to them?

We thus have two approaches to empowerment for the poor: "Up by your own bootstraps" model, and the 1960s Maximum Feasible Participation/Manipulation model. These are competing views on what is possible with the poor, and neither presents a particularly flattering image: one suggests the poor are lazy, and their lack of empowerment is due to their own lack of effort, and the second suggests the poor are pawns and may not actually know what is best for them. Though there are likely to be, indeed most definitely are, subsets of the population of poor people who reside at these extremes, most, we suggest, are in the middle somewhere: hard working, eager for comfort if not success, and capable of self-empowerment and self-presentation of interests without manipulative hand-holding or prodding.

The democratic dilemma of empowerment is this: Manipulation of any kind is not empowerment; it represents a "power over" the poor and disaffected. Empowerment is a "power with" the poor (Follett 1918). Achieving the second may require partaking in the former, thus risking a state of permanent manipulation. Power, then, becomes an illusion.

To avoid this fate, we must understand what can lead the masses, poor or otherwise, to neither seek nor accept power offered to them. We can consider five reasons: (1) non-blissful ignorance, (2) fear of failure, (3) fear of status loss, (4) lack of interest, or (5) lack of time.

Saul Alinksy (1989) develops his principles or rules for community organizing partially on the assumption that those without power did not understand their limitations, or, to use Freire's (2011) language, the extent of their oppression. Alinsky and Freire operate with essentially the same starting point: those who would empower must teach the lack of power by allowing the free exercise of power. Power parceled out and controlled is manipulated power. As such, the powerless might neither seek nor accept power if they do not, to put it blandly, know what they are missing. To empower with, or have power with "us"/the poor, then requires education that awakens the mind and overall consciousness to the lack of power that exists and the life limitations that accompany this lack of power. This ignorance is not blissful; it perpetuates powerlessness such that the lack of power is not understood, and powerlessness or manipulation is an accepted way of life.

Not accepting or seeking power may also be grounded in fear: fear of failure and, related, fear of status loss. To accept and use power is to seek change; change is uncertain and potentially scary, even change away from a life of material poverty. To use power and fail potentially sets the person or group of people back, in the same manner as taking initiative to participate in some democratic process only to find that influence is limited. The person is potentially more likely to drop out after the failed or negative experience (Bryer 2011).

Following implementation of Maximum Feasible Participation of the poor in the 1960s and 1970s, public opinion turned against the poor; they were labeled as greedy and lazy, entitled without work ethic, or even societal parasites. This was partially a function of the adversarial strategies employed by community poor advocates, or the self-appointed representatives. To the extent the poor used power, their status shifted, not from the forgotten to the cared for but from the forgotten to the despised. To know that such a stereotype exists makes pursuit of power a somewhat risky proposition—emotionally, psychologically, and potentially physically.

The final reasons for not pursuing power are grounded in lack of time and lack of interest. The working poor may very well have limited time, between work obligations and family obligations, to engage in any meaningful way such that their lot can improve through a combination of projects and initiatives of government and nonprofit organizations and personal effort. Lack of interest is a product of powerlessness and might be reversed once genuine power is achieved and utilized without manipulative action by outsiders.

Responsiveness

The poor might be powerful, they might have capacity for self-presentation, but to complete the circle and ensure low status poverty and low agency poverty, government officials and nonprofit leaders must also be responsive to the poor. In other words, the poor must be perceived not only as powerful and capable but also as credible. The demands and expectations of the poor must be seen as legitimate and worthy of response.

Responsiveness, perhaps what we can consider a close cousin of representation (Bryer and Sahin 2012), is multifaceted in the same way as power and representation. It requires not only felt and actual discretion on the part of the government or nonprofit officials who have the charge of delivering (or not delivering) services to the poor, but it requires as well a desire to deliver those services—to substantively represent through actions that meet the expressed or implied needs of the poor.

We can conceptualize five variants of responsiveness (Bryer 2007):

- Constrained
- Dictated
- Entrepreneurial
- Purposive
- Collaborative

Constrained responsiveness assumes the individual has no or very limited discretion regarding the application of a law or policy. Policy implementation responses are hardwired into legislative language. For instance, individual or family eligibility for certain goods or services is specifically established through statute. Dictated responsiveness similarly limits individual discretion in policy implementation, as elected officials or politically appointed officials provide high levels of oversight. The discretion for responsiveness, then, exists at the political level.

Entrepreneurial responsiveness assumes the policy implementer has a certain amount of discretion, specifically to take risks in pursuit of agreed upon policy objectives. For instance, if there exists a policy goal to increase housing for the homeless, an administrator in a public agency or nonprofit professional will have the latitude to seek and experiment with solutions independent or with loose oversight from political officials.

Purposive responsiveness similarly affords great discretion to the implementer, who is driven not by adherence to rules but achievement of personally motivating goals: end homelessness, feed nutritious meals to all children, or, even, ensure no waste, fraud or abuse in the expenditure of public monies. Negative perceptions of the poor by those who have power and discretion to be responsive can lead to low levels of responsiveness to individual need while ensuring responsiveness to other stakeholders.

This is the fundamental dilemma with the idea of responsiveness. There are many stakeholders with potentially equally legitimate interests that can be the focus of positive response or target of negative response. Thus, the final form of responsiveness (Bryer 2007) is collaborative responsiveness through which a policy implementer convenes a dialogic process with diverse stakeholders and commits to act and respond in a way that is the consensus view or decision of the group.

For this process to work, as a measure of responsiveness, it requires more than tokenistic participation of the poor or manipulation rather than empowerment of the poor. Will the poor have more than a symbolic seat at the table? Will they be dismissed as salient advisors on matters concerning the economy or other issues? This is a question of participation and what "maximum feasible participation" actually entails. We close this chapter by applying these three dimensions of representation, power, and responsiveness to Maximum Feasible Participation as it has been implemented in prior conceptions.

Application to Maximum Feasible Participation

Daniel Patrick Moynihan served in the Kennedy, Johnson, Nixon, and Ford administrations, and later served as U.S. Senator from New York for twenty-four years. In 1969, he summarized four distinct conceptions of Maximum Feasible Participation: (1) *organize the power* structure by creating mechanisms for cooperation across existing government, nonprofit, and private sector organizations, (2) *expand the power* structure by developing opportunities for citizens with low income to enter the professional workforce, (3) *confront the power* structure by redistributing power through democratization processes, and (4) *assisting the power* structure by creating formal representation on boards or advisory councils for low-income citizens. Each of these conceptions is re-presented through the lens of representation, power, and responsiveness theories.

Organizing the power structure, on its own, maintains an implied assumption that the poor are clients for service delivery agencies and without a role in shaping policy or delivering programs or services. The poor are powerless as the professional class agency personnel administer programs to and for the poor. Self-appointed representatives as professional class public servants in public and nonprofit sectors, primarily, attempt to meet the needs of the poor based on professional norms, requisite policies, and individual personal expert preferences. The intent of coordinating across multiple service delivery agencies and sectors is to enhance responsiveness, at least in terms expressed by the professional elite. Overall, then, representation is dependent on the self-appointed without clear accountability mechanisms, empowerment of the poor is low, and responsiveness is high within a purposive or entrepreneurial frame and not a collaborative frame.

Expanding the power structure seeks to help the poor by facilitating their entry and staying power within the job market. How this is accomplished may or may not include ideas from the poor themselves but rather policy and economic elites who "pull the levers" of the economy (e.g., fiscal policy including tax rates, incentives, credits, and deductions) to help spur investment, new business development, and existing business expansion. If this lever pulling is successful, the poor will gain access to more and better financial opportunities, thus helping them shed the stigma of subsistence poverty, reduce status poverty, and potentially reduce agency poverty. In so doing, the ability for the poor-turned-less poor to self-present their interests expands; power increases, and responsiveness potentially goes up. However, if the expansion of the power structure happens *to* the poor rather than *with* the poor, the "dignity" and empowerment that come with entering the decently paid workforce may not reflect the values and interests beyond financial interests of the population. The economy will be re-created to help the poor through the efforts of self-appointed representatives; preparing the poor-turned-less poor into capable citizens without prior inclusion in political or policy processes potentially then becomes problematic.

Confronting the power structure specifically aims to empower by establishing adversarial relationships between those without power—the poor—and those with power. In so doing, the impact on the multiple forms of poverty might be negligible or opposite that intended. Subsistence poverty might be reduced or mitigated through gaining access to more services and resources (e.g., food stamps, worker training, etc.), but status and agency poverty might suffer. This is so, particularly if the poor are not truly empowered but are manipulated. Representation leads to self-presentation but potentially with the "strings" being pulled by elites from outside, directing the poor to behave and demand services in particular ways, using particular language, and at particular moments in time. Short-term responsiveness to demands might increase, but as was demonstrated with the actual implementation of this form of Maximum Feasible Participation, the high status poverty resulting from adversarial rather than empowered collaborative behavior might ultimately lead to policies and programs that reduce responsiveness or erect barriers to responsiveness, as responsiveness becomes almost exclusively rule-bound and constrained.

Assisting the power structure can be similarly ambiguous as confronting the power structure. Through this approach, the poor are given a seat at the table, or at least true representatives of the poor, meaning individuals selected from the population of poor people through some mechanism, either elected or appointed, or some combination of the two. As such there is substantive representation, but the representation might be tokenistic and not empowering. If the poor are not the only and final decision-makers on matters affecting them, then their voice is one of many. That being the case, responsiveness is of a collaborative kind, where decision-makers hear viewpoints from multiple perspectives. Without full empowerment to the full population, however, this responsiveness may still be dominated by

Table 3.1. Maximum Feasible Participation and Representation, Power, and Responsiveness

	Representation	Power	Responsiveness
Organizing the Power Structure	Self-appointed without clear accountability	Low or no empowerment	Increased responsiveness that is purposive and entrepreneurial
Expanding the Power Structure	Version 1: Self-presentation becomes possible Version 2: Self-appointed with possibility of future accountability	Version 1: Power increases with more financial stake in society Version 2: Increased power without preparation for its use	Version 1: Increased responsiveness that is entrepreneurial and collaborative Version 2: No change in responsiveness
Confronting the Power Structure	Self-presentation with strings	Increase in power but with possible manipulation	Potentially reduced responsiveness with reduced status, or responsiveness increased based on rules and program eligibility
Assisting the Power Structure	Limited self-presentation	Limited, tokenistic power	Increased restricted collaborative responsiveness

elites who represent their own interests without necessarily developing a full understanding or appreciation for the interests of the poor. Table 3.1 summarizes these conceptions of Maximum Feasible Participation according to the elements of power, responsiveness, and representation.

In the next chapter, we look more deeply at this question of representation than we already have. As representation and the ability to self-present is central to the capacity of the poor and non-poor to fully, comprehensively, and with fully understood bias create and implement solutions to reducing poverty in all of its forms.

CHAPTER FOUR

~

Representation of the Included-In and Included-Out

In this chapter, we build on a theme introduced in the third chapter and assess assumptions regarding the capacity of individuals and collectives to represent self and represent other. Are those experiencing poverty the best to represent their own interests? Are those who have never experienced poverty capable of addressing the needs and advocating for the interests of the poor? The lines between included-in, included-out, and excluded citizens will be made at once clear within this chapter but also potentially muddled as the subjectivity of who belongs in what category is identified as one of the critical issues preventing a societal "attack" on poverty in all of its forms.

To represent, as we discussed previously, is to act or vote on behalf of another. Government officials, elected, appointed, and career, as a matter of course, make decisions and act for the multitude and subsets of the masses on a regular basis. The legitimacy of this representation relies on the consent of those who are represented, or the consent, in this case, of the governed. As written in the U.S. Declaration of Independence, governments derive their "just powers from the consent of the governed." The British monarch in 1776 was not seen to have received such consent from American colonists, thus giving cause to the rebellion and revolution.

Consent, in political philosophy, is considered granted through majority will as expressed through the vote, or through silent acquiescence to government rule, at least insofar as there exist genuine opportunities for citizens to challenge said rule through protest or other forms of public participation (Cooper, Bryer, and Meek, 2006), or more formal recall elections in certain scenarios. This, however, is a rather weak form of consent, as it is based on individual and mass perception of desire and may not be, indeed is likely not, informed. The requirements for a researcher to conduct an interview with a citizen are more onerous, as the citizen must provide "informed consent" attesting that she understands the purpose of the research, risks involved, and any/all rights responsibilities. In the act of voting, there is no such requirement or anything resembling even such an expectation.

Indeed, scholars and philosophers dating to antiquity have questioned the ability of individuals and then masses of individuals to be informed. Ignorance and emotionality were considered by the founders of the United States to be the norm, and so systems of government needed to be created to, in the words of Alexander Hamilton and James Madison, protect the people from themselves and allow for more cool and sedate discussion and reflection on the issues facing the people and the country as a whole (Bryer and Cooper 2012).

For legitimate representation to occur, the represented must be able to hold the representatives to account; the people must be able to hold the government to account. Such accountability is possible only if the represented are informed at least in a general way; the represented must be informed enough to be able to interpret whether the representatives are acting in their interests, in the interests of another, or in self-interest for themselves. If such discernment is not possible given lack of information there can be no true consent, even if the people vote for one candidate instead of another or one political party instead of another. If the vote is not informed, any action that results from the accumulation of votes is not consensual. The representation is not legitimate, as the lack of informed decision-making renders holding representatives accountable problematic, to say the least.

Short of discarding the whole notion of democratic accountability as an idealist's dream, these issues do reveal substantive challenges to enabling representation of the interests of the poor. To consider these challenges, we unpack the relationships between included-in and included-out citizens, or the relationship between those who might be representatives and their represented, respectively.

First, within the population of included-in citizens, there are confounding relationships that speak to the kinds of responsibility citizens might feel in their interactions with others. To argue this point, we use a metaphorical tale from Rabbi Lau-Lavie told on the National Public Radio program, *On Being*. The rabbi told the tale to his interviewer and the program's host, Krista Tippett, during a discussion of building relationships together as a people, across divisions. He said (Lau-Lavie 2017):

It's this Talmudic parable about a ship that is sailing, and there are many cabins. And one of the people in the cabins on the lower floor decides to dig a hole in the floor of his cabin, and does so, and sure enough, the ship begins to sink. And the other passengers suddenly discover what's going on and see this guy with a hole in the floor. And they say, "What are you doing?" And he says, "Well, it's my cabin. I paid for it." And down goes the ship.

He continued, relating the discussion to the American presidential election of 2016, which saw divisions within society manifest in multiple ways (Lau-Lavie 2017):

And it's a story in the Talmud that talks about human responsibility in the Jewish sense—that we're all in the same ship together. But I've been wrestling with it and . . . talking about what does it mean for us to be that person? And where have we been only focusing on my cabin and me-me-me-me-me-me-me-me-me-me, and where are we not part of a "we"? And how is that true of every single one of us, and how that is true in some ways of America, and how the narcissistic, me-focused, insight-driven, my own needs and aspirations in this age have taken so hold of us that the sense of public and communal and responsible-for-other, including the limping and the weak at the edges of our camp, in some way has not been looked at as religious traditions have taught us to and as the Bible again and again reminds us: "Remember the Other. Remember the Other. You were the Other." And then the question is, what is the "we," because the boundaries of what is "we" are shifting.

In the group of included-in citizens, at least within the United States, individuals are not properly socialized, to use a phrase from Amitai Etzioni (1994). They focus on "I" but neglect the "we." Like the man on the boat who drills a hole because it is his cabin, as he has a right to do with his property, citizens tend to be self-interested first.

Within the "privileged" population of included-in citizens, the "I" dominates and remains dominant through social isolation, concern for appearing to not fit into the group, and desire to not lose status—similar issues that we previously considered as preventing the powerless from seeking or accepting power. It is better, in this context, to remain silent or to blend into the masses than to exert civic energy that rocks the communal boat. Indeed, in American society, it is more palatable it seems to preserve discretion of private property use that results in a slow sinking of the boat rather than to engage in political action that causes some nausea but ultimately keeps everyone afloat (Somin 2010; Riley-Smith 2010).

Atomistic individualism of the included-in population complicates the question of representation. Fundamentally, and a bit rhetorically, how can the self-obsessed and self-interested person be shaped or open themselves to express concern for others, especially when the others exist on a lower social and economic plane? How can the included-in develop a sense of obligation towards the included-out? And, the reverse, how can the included-out populations open themselves to be represented wholly and fully, and, ideally, on the way towards self-empowerment?

The alert reader will observe in the previous paragraph the use of the singular in referring to the included-in, and the use of the plural in referring to the included-out. The included-in are considered here as a cohesive whole, and the included-out as individuals. Writing in such a way was not intentional, but the interpretation of this cognitive "blunder" can be quite significant when considering the challenge before us.

Use of such phrasing presents a paradox. The included-in are defined by their individualism, and yet I approach them as a collective whole. The included-out are, as we discussed in previous chapters, lumped together and stereotyped, denied their individuality; yet, I approach them as individuals. This "accident" of writing is logical and accurate. The included-in cherish their individuality, but social norms and desire to belong limit their willingness to act on their freedom. If any of the group wished to break from the pack, they would risk being ostracized.

Here is a short example of that: in a community of approximately 75,000 people in Florida, a local homeowners association initiated a process to determine if the community could incorporate or become an independent city. At the time of the example, the community was unincorporated and spread across two counties. The community was quite diverse, with working class Hispanics living in the interior of the community, more wealthy gated communities on the periphery, and there was even a nudist "colony." One of the gated communities was designated as for those aged fifty-five and older, an active adult community. Residents of this community were strongly opposed to incorporation, partially for fear that becoming a City would permit local authorities to open the gates of their living area, which includes swimming pools and golf courses, to the Spanish-speaking, working class masses. Legally, this was not possible, but the fear was spurred on by rumor (Bryer 2010).

The included-in population residing in the active adult gated community formed a cohesive whole, protecting their individual property and hard-earned livelihood by effectively demonizing those who were included-out literally outside their gates. The example of the paradox comes in the form of a small group within the gated community who chose to speak on behalf of the whole—those included-in inside the gates and those included-out outside the gates. One gentleman was booed loudly when speaking at a meeting with 500 or more of his neighbors, leading his doctor to advise that he cease all activity related to the question of incorporation (Bryer 2010). The included-in citizen who exercised individuality to align with the "other" was in fact ostracized.

Whereas the included-in are "one," the included-out, to achieve a status of personal identity apart from the pack and free from the stereotype, require individuality to be perceived and recognized by society. The included-out are many; they are materially poor, refugees, migrants, mentally challenged, physically challenged, with family obligations, without family obligations, urban dwellers, rural residents, suburbanites, drug addicted, substance free, hard working, and/or lazy.

The individual must emerge from the included-out pack to enjoy the benefits of the included-in collective. This means that the included-in must have true individual discretion and power to break from the mold in order to represent others, and the included-out must have empowerment to demonstrate their true selves, such that the "deserving" poor can be separated from the "undeserving" poor and the legitimately lazy not confused with the perseverant who are beaten down. The democratic dilemma is solved when these individual and population movements or empowerments are achieved, and we are free from manipulation of the masses through peer or group pressure or through blind, irrational empathy.

In chapters 5–7, we identify past, current, and potential future strategies to reach this solution. Before proceeding, though, a few additional words on empathy are in order. Empathy, as a construct that can facilitate one person acting for or representing another, is a potential bridge between the included-in and included-out within society. It is "a kind of vicarious emotion: it's feeling what one takes another person to be feeling" (Prinz 2011, 212).

As we discuss in chapter 3, such empathy or feeling may not be a positive attribute; indeed, empathy so construed is subject to emotional manipulation (Bloom 2016), which may serve to treat a small part of a broader societal problem while neglecting those parts that do not emotionally move us as individuals in such way.

When I teach about Ursula Le Guin's fictional city of Omelas (from the second chapter), I show an image of a clearly malnourished small child—the child in the cellar—with bones showing, shallow eyes, and I speak the words Le Guin writes about the child. I describe how the city's residents occasionally enter the cellar and throw food at it. Whether my audience is a room full of students or a large hall of community practitioners, the reaction of the people is palpable. Some look away; some look at me in confusion, their eyes asking, "Why are you showing such a horrible picture?" The image combined with the words has the intended effect; I time-and-again manipulate my students and others to think about ethics or think about civics in a way they have not considered it before. If I asked them to donate money to help starving children at that moment, some if not most would probably do so; if I asked them to commit to volunteering at a homeless shelter for youth, most would probably do so.

This is precisely what happens when the included-in are presented with powerful images in photographs, words, or some other artistic form. Showing the lifeless body of a small refugee boy washed up on shore led to an outpouring of support for refugee-serving organizations (Bloch 2015). Pleas for

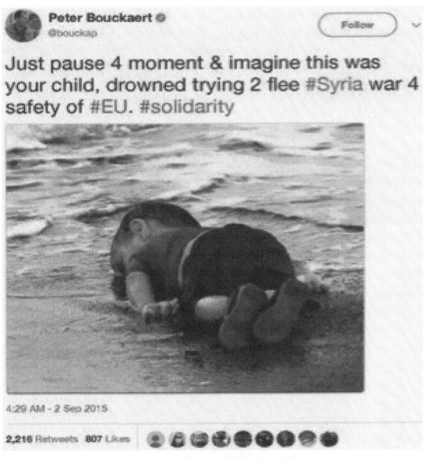

Figure 4.1.   Tweet about the Refugee Boy Washed Up on Shore

compassion spread throughout the Internet and in traditional media, such as seen in figure 4.1, a Twitter post from Peter Bouckaert, Emergency Director at Human Rights Watch.

Support dried up in large measure after the memory of the image faded from consciousness. This is the downside of empathy as mobilizer of action; it is short-lived, narrowly defined, and exclusionary (Bloom 2016). It is good for short-term fundraising but bad for a long-term . . . war on poverty and impoverished citizenship, as it were. In developing the strategies for this war and thinking about building sustainable and strong bridges across the included-in and the included-out, we can consider the suggestion from Prinz (2011, 229): "When confronted with moral offences, it's not enough to commiserate with victims. We should get uppity."

In the next several chapters, we consider how uppity can happen, how bridges can be built, and how subsistence, agency, and status poverties can be attacked. We begin with a review of past efforts to fight poverty in the United States (chapters 5 and 6), followed by introduction of defined proposals for fighting the war today and in the future (chapter 7), the battle in the context of refugees and migrants (chapter 8), and global perspectives on the question (chapter 9).

CHAPTER FIVE

∿

Historical Development of Poverty Policies

Social scientists, politicians, and public administrators have long debated about how social policies should be designed to address poverty in communities. The causes of poverty are complex and intersectional. Goodin and Le Grand (1987) argue "the failure of social policies to reduce inequality lies in the beneficial participation of the nonpoor in the welfare state" (as cited in Korpi and Palme 1998, 4). While providing poor people with money, affordable housing, education and job opportunities, the policy should also empower citizens, by ensuring their participation in social and economic processes that address needs in communities.

This and the next chapter accomplishes three objectives: (1) understand the historical development and evolution of policies to reduce poverty in all its forms in the United States, as enacted, and (2) present through a case study of one program, the Community Development Block Grant, the theory and philosophy behind one prominent policy, and the political calculus that leads to the creation of certain programs, and (3) consider other issues in the contemporary debate on poverty and anti-poverty policies in the United States.

Policies to address poverty can be categorized both by substantive focus and also by function. Substantive focus options have been person-centered or place-based (Lewis and Alexander 2015); functions have consisted of protection or promotion of the poor (Ravallion 2013). Person-centered policies are those that provide direct cash or non-cash assistance to an individual or family; place-based policies focus on lifting neighborhoods or communities through targeted programs. Protection policies provide support for individuals, directly or indirectly, for when they fall on hard times, trying to prevent hunger and homelessness; promotion policies try to provide opportunities to enable poor individuals to escape poverty.

By providing opportunities to become more financially stable and even rise into a higher economic class, promotion policies implicitly if not explicitly address agency and status poverty as well as subsistence poverty. They are strategies of expanding the power structure (see chapter 3). Protection policies only address subsistence poverty. Without explicit objective to address agency and status poverty, however, promotion policies may likely fail to empower. To give a person a car does not mean he will know how to drive; to lead a person to water does not mean she will know how to fish. In the same manner, to enable opportunity financially does not mean a person will be ready to engage in democratic discourse to self-present their interests or represent the interests of others; they may not be able to transition from included-out to included-in status within society.

In the following pages, we review poverty policies in the United States up until 2017. Table 5.1 lists most prominent policies according to these substantive foci and functions; the list is illustrative and not exhaustive.

Table 5.1.   Summary of Poverty Policies by Substantive Focus and Function

	Protection	Promotion
Person-Centered	Aid to Families with Dependent Children (AFDC)	Child Tax Credit (CTC)
	Supplemental Nutrition Assistance Program (SNAP)	Earned Income Tax Credit (EITC)
	Women, Infants & Children (WIC)	Minimum Wage
	Housing Vouchers	Temporary Assistance to Needy Families (TANF)
	Social Security	Job Training Programs*
	Medicare	Head Start*
	Medicaid	HighScope/Perry Preschool*
		Education Vouchers/Loans/Tax Credits*
Place-Based	[Not Applicable]	HOPE VI Mixed-Income Communities (Choice Neighborhoods Initiative)*
		Neighborhood Revitalization Initiative (Harlem Children's Zone)*
		Area Redevelopment Act
		Appalachian Regional Development Act
		Volunteers in Service to America (VISTA)*
		Community Action Program (CAP)*

Programs and policies are indicated with a "*" symbol to indicate the potential for empowerment to occur, which, for the purposes of this assessment, is defined as potentially addressing agency or status poverty (in chapter 7, we define empowerment more robustly). Relatively few programs or policies have the potential for empowerment, and those that do, we will consider, have not been successful in fulfilling that potential. We consider each cell and the programs and policies within each. Items in the table are not listed in any particular order.

Person-Centered Protection Policies and Programs

Programs and policies listed here are substantively focused on meeting needs of individuals or families so that they will mitigate suffering through hunger or homelessness. They are direct cash or non-cash assistance programs that have sought to stabilize a situation for an individual or family enduring financial hardship; they are not intended to help lift the person or family out of the impoverished situation but only to control the situation such that it does not get materially worse. Programs and policies in this category include but might not be limited to, in no particular order:

- Aid to Families with Dependent Children (AFDC)
- Supplemental Nutrition Assistance Program (SNAP)
- Women, Infants & Children (WIC)
- Housing Vouchers
- Social Security
- Medicare
- Medicaid

Aid to Families with Dependent Children (AFDC)
The Social Security Act of 1935 established Aid to Families with Dependent Children (AFDC) as a means to protect children whose mother or father was "absent from the home, incapacitated, deceased, or unemployed" (United States Department of Health and Human Services 2009). Forged in the context of the Great Depression, the welfare program transferred funds from the federal government to state governments to support families with children. The program remained in place officially until passage of the Personal Responsibility and Work Reconciliation Act of 1996 and establishment of Temporary Assistance for Needy Families (TANF). AFDC came under attack leading up to its replacement as a source of dependency for the

poor, thus emerging work requirements and lifetime limits on support provided through TANF. The program was fundamentally a protection program, providing neither incentive nor requirement to leave the welfare rolls and pursue work opportunities.

Supplemental Nutrition to Needy Families (SNAP)

As described by the United States Department of Agriculture (2017):

> SNAP offers nutrition assistance to millions of eligible, low-income individuals and families and provides economic benefits to communities. SNAP is the largest program in the domestic hunger safety net. The Food and Nutrition Service works with State agencies, nutrition educators, and neighborhood and faith-based organizations to ensure that those eligible for nutrition assistance can make informed decisions about applying for the program and can access benefits.

The food stamp program was first formally authorized as a pilot project based on an Executive Order of President John F. Kennedy in 1961, a program that was made permanent in 1964 with passage of the Food Stamp Act. Within ten years, the program expanded to all fifty states and territories in the United States. From there, modifications to the program were made, including establishment of national eligibility standards in 1977, creation of the Electronic Benefits Transfer (EBT) system in 1984 that enabled individuals to use a debit-like card rather than stamps to purchase food, and renaming of the food stamp program in 2008 to its current title: SNAP (United States Department of Agriculture 2017b).

As a protection program to ensure adults and children have the opportunity to eat nutritious meals, the program has shown positive results. Specifically related to poverty, according to the Census Bureau, SNAP lifted 5 million individuals, including 2.2 million children, out of poverty in 2012. There are some work or job training requirements to receiving SNAP benefits, which have the potential to be promotional if a good, stable job is found.

Women, Infants, and Children (WIC)

WIC is another food and nutrition program that specifically targets pregnant women, infants, and children up to age five. The program ensures access to a healthy diet, which can facilitate a healthier life and better life outcomes. "The Special Supplemental Nutrition Program for Women, Infants, and Children—better known as the WIC Program—serves to safeguard the health of low-income pregnant, postpartum, and breastfeeding women, infants, and children up to age five who are at nutritional risk by providing nutritious foods to supplement diets, information on healthy eating including breastfeeding promotion and support, and referrals to health care" (United States Department of Agriculture 2016).

Housing Vouchers

Section 8 housing is the dominant form of individually focused assistance to put low-income individuals into stable housing. It is a housing voucher program that helps individuals pay for housing in the private market. As of May 2017, more than 5 million people in 2.2 million low-income families use vouchers (Center for Budget and Policy Priorities 2017). Rather than housing people directly in publicly owned housing, this program gives the individual and family choice as to where they live, with impacts being a reduction in potential homelessness and the opportunity for low-income individuals to move out of fully impoverished neighborhoods.

Social Security

The advent of social security has a rich history that can be traced to economic security programs of the ancient Greeks (Social Security Administration 2017). Formally, the social security as economic security was established in the United States through the Social Security Act of 1935, the preamble of which reads:

> An act to provide for the general welfare by establishing a system of Federal old-age benefits, and by enabling the several States to make more adequate provision for aged persons, blind persons, dependent and crippled children, maternal and child welfare, public health, and the administration of their un-employment compensation laws; to establish a Social Security Board; to raise revenue; and for other purposes.

Born in the Great Depression, this program has kept vast numbers of people and families out of poverty, particularly with a growth in benefits provided during the Johnson administration. Since that time, the program has not been without critics; the financial sustainability of the program has been questioned as a smaller workforce pays into the system to meet the needs of retirees. There have been active debates to privatize the system, including through investment of collected funds in stock or bond markets, as well as to raise the eligibility age for receiving benefits given expectations of longer lifespans. The program has persisted as designed and has served its purpose, providing cash support to those who are in need or might be at risk of being in need.

Medicare and Medicaid

Medicare and Medicaid were established in 1965, established through a law signed by President Johnson. The initial law provided Hospital Insurance and Medical Insurance; the scope and breadth of the law has evolved since this time. Medicare now covers the disabled, those aged sixty-five and over who choose to have coverage, and others. It also provides coverage for prescription drugs. Medicaid covers low-income families, pregnant women, people with disabilities, and people in need of long-term care. Like other anti-poverty programs, individual states design their own Medicaid programs, which has allowed some to accept Medicaid expansion to the poor and some to decline this expansion under the terms of the Affordable Care Act, signed in 2010 by President Obama. A final program within this family of programs is the Children's Health Insurance Program (CHIP), created in 1997 by President Clinton, providing insurance to uninsured children. These are protection programs that try to ensure individuals and families will have access to the care they need, despite their economic status.

Person-Centered Promotion Policies and Programs

Programs and policies listed here are targeted to individuals and families with defined need and eligibility for support. Unlike the programs and policies outlined in the previous category, these have a clear objective to not only alleviate direct suffering through limited finances but to ideally propel an individual or family out of poverty so that they can create a self-sustaining future free from support. Programs and policies include:

- Child Tax Credit (CTC)
- Earned Income Tax Credit (EITC)
- Minimum Wage
- Temporary Assistance to Needy Families (TANF)
- Job Training Programs*
- Head Start*
- HighScope/Perry Preschool
- Education Vouchers/Loans/Tax Credits

Child Tax Credit and Earned Income Tax Credit

The Child Tax Credit (CTC) and Earned Income Tax Credit (EITC) are cash assistance programs that offer support to eligible individuals upon filing of annual taxes. Hungerford and Thiess (2013, 2) summarize the attributes of these two programs:

- Claiming the EITC and CTC can be complicated and involves filing additional tax forms, which leads to errors of both over- and underpayment.
- The EITC appears to increase the labor force participation of single mothers, yet the high marginal tax rates associated with its phase-out range do not appear to have a significant work disincentive effect.
- The EITC is, by far, the most progressive tax expenditure in the income tax code.
- The EITC reduces poverty significantly, with children constituting half of the individuals it lifts out of poverty.
- The EITC and CTC are effective in increasing after-tax income of targeted groups, reducing poverty, and reducing income inequality.

To be eligible for the EITC, a person must file taxes and report income. As such, there is a built in work incentive to the system. The credit is designed in such a way such that if the credit leads to a negative amount in taxes owed, it will be paid as a refund to the tax filer. EITC was first enacted in 1975 and expanded and made permanent by the Revenue Act of 1978. As of 2012, the maximum credit is $5,891 for a household with three children, with a lower credit for households with fewer children or no children. It is designed to help mostly to support families to provide opportunity for children, as the maximum credit for no children in 2012 was $475. Eligibility is based on income, where any income above $0 qualifies a filer for the credit, with the amount of credit increasing to a specified amount depending on the number of filers (e.g., single, married) and number of children, and then decreasing for each additional dollar of income until a maximum eligibility salary is reached. At that point, the filer(s) are not eligible for any credit. As of 2012, the maximum salary, for instance, for a married couple with two children to receive the EITC was $47,162.

The CTC was created in 1997 as a partially refundable tax credit with income conditions of $400 per child in a household. This amount was increased to $1,000 per child in 2003. The credit is intended for families across income levels up to a certain amount (e.g., $150,000 adjusted gross income for a married couple). It is a fixed credit amount per child and does not adjust downward for additional children after the first. The credit is in addition to the dependent tax exemption that reduces overall taxable income.

According to Hungerford and Thiess (2013), the combined EITC and CTC have had measurable impact on poverty. One estimate suggests nearly 6 million people are not poor, by the official definition, in 2011 because of these credits. The EITC lifts families with children out of poverty but, generally, not single or married filers without children.

Minimum Wage

The first federal minimum wage was established in 1938 with occasional increases every five to ten years. The most recent increase came in 2009 and is currently set at $7.25 per hour. Individual States and Cities, with some exceptions, can establish a higher minimum wage than the federal minimum. The impact on poverty of the minimum wage is mixed, or at least formal evaluations of the impact produce mixed findings. As with tax credits, the impact will depend on family composition, number of children, number of hours worked per week, and other costs associated with the job, such as transportation. The minimum wage is not calculated using any specific formula and is more the result of political compromise than economic science; it is not pegged to inflation and so requires an act of Congress to increase it. The minimum wage is most clearly not a living wage, which would, if the worker is full time, propel the individual to an income level that is not poverty level.

The argument for a minimum, or indeed a living, wage is partially to make employment pay. In other words, with all other government programs and policies that provide cash and non-cash assistance to the poor, it can work out that an individual will be worse off with a full time or less job than to receive social support. Without an appropriately set minimum wage or a livable wage, there are personal disincentives to get a job and to become self-sufficient. Thus, in the City of Los Angeles now, the minimum wage is set at a more livable standard of $15 per hour, well above the federal minimum. New York State is moving in the same direction, and other cities have experimented with similar, though with mixed results.

There are multiple concerns of critics of a minimum or livable wage. One is that by forcing employers to pay higher wages, they will be forced to reduce their workforce, thus employing fewer people, or they may choose to invest in automation or new technology to replace workers entirely, thus reducing employment. There is also a concern that increasing wages at the bottom will lead to increased wages marginally at higher income levels; the overall income inequality may reduce, but the income gap will persist, and with potential price inflation due to higher wages across the board, the spending power of the bottom tier will remain comparatively low and only marginally better than exists today. As such, critics question whether the cost of potential reduced overall employment in low or no skill jobs is worth any marginal gain in spending power and marginal reduction in income inequality.

Temporary Assistance for Needy Families

Temporary Assistance for Needy Families (TANF) replaced Aid for Families with Dependent Children (AFDC) as part of welfare reform enacted through the Personal Responsibility and Work Opportunity Reconciliation Act of 1996. As discussed previously, AFDC provided cash welfare to poor families with children since 1935. TANF decentralized the program and gave more control to states for designing welfare programs that meet the needs of the poor; it accomplished this by creating block grants for the states while requiring essentially a match of a certain calculated amount for the amount received through the grant.

TANF has four goals, which can be addressed through state use of the funds: (1) provide assistance to needy families so that children may be cared for in their own homes or in the homes of relatives, (2) end the dependence of needy parents on government benefits by promoting job preparation, work, and marriage, (3) prevent and reduce the incidence of out of wedlock pregnancies and establish annual numerical goals for preventing and reducing the incidence of these pregnancies, and (4) encourage the formation and maintenance of two parent families. These goals are each aligned with social science that suggests factors that prevent families from escaping poverty are broken families, single parent homes, unplanned pregnancy, and preparation for work (Center for Budget and Policy Priorities 2015).

With their block grant discretion, states can establish their own programs and eligibility for programs according to their needs and interests. However, one substantial change that affects the individual receiving aid, compared to aid dispensed through AFDC, are a work requirement and lifetime limit on assistance received. TANF funds cannot be given to a family with an adult present for more than sixty months, except for 20 percent of cases due to exceptional hardship. Funds cannot be provided to or used for a legal immigrant except until they have been in the United States for at least five years. Individuals receiving support must also be engaged in some kind of work activity, either employed or actively seeking employment, defined by the states with federally defined parameters. States can use their own, non-federal funding to supplement or provide support beyond federal restrictions and parameters; they can also establish more rigorous restrictions with their own money.

TANF is listed with a promotion, rather than a protection, function due to the work requirement and lifetime limits for receiving support, contrasted with AFDC. The philosophy and possible theory is that an individual will respond to these restrictions and be more likely to seek full or near full-time employment and move towards self-sufficiency. Time limits and work requirements force able-bodied individuals to not be dependent on direct cash or non-cash assistance.

In practice, this works when the economy is strong and the job market is healthy with low unemployment. However, during a recession, the work requirements and time limits become a potential impediment to protection, let alone providing a possibility for promotion (Center for Budget and Policy Priorities 2015). As a result, the cash assistance dominated welfare system supported by AFDC has largely been replaced in the anti-poverty policy patchwork with tax credits and non-cash assistance for specific quality of life protections, such as Supplemental Nutrition Assistance Program (SNAP) benefits (Bane 2009).

Job Training Programs

There are numerous examples of federally funded job training programs dating to 1962 that have sought to provide skills to poor and unemployed citizens, such that they will have the opportunity to enter into higher-skilled employment, establish professional relationships, and move towards inclusion in other aspects of society (O'Leary, Straits, and Wandner 2004).

The first job training program of note was the Manpower Development and Training Act (MDTA), established in 1962. This program was designed for on-the-job training for low income and welfare recipients. Funding was provided to local agencies based on a fixed formula and through competition. The program was never fully evaluated before being disbanded in 1969, largely for administrative reasons (O'Leary et al. 2004).

Another example was created by the Economic Opportunity Act of 1964, which was the central War on Poverty legislation that established numerous anti-poverty programs, mostly coordinated by the newly established Office of Economic Opportunity (OEO). Job Corps is a one year residential program for disadvantaged youth that provides job training and remedial learning for academic success. Evaluations of Job Corps have found positive impacts. According to Burghardt et al. (2017): "[E]arnings gains, educational progress, and other positive changes were found across most groups of participants and are expected to persist as they get older."

The Comprehensive Employment and Training Act of 1973 established local advisory boards to develop training programs fit to specific localities. This decentralization was designed to ensure greatest responsiveness to all three groups previously served by other programs, namely economically disadvantaged, welfare recipients, and disadvantaged youth. This program ended following some scandal regarding the use of funds and service to ineligible individuals (O'Leary et al. 2004).

By the early 1990s, there were 163 distinct job training programs funded by various agencies of the federal government. Some of these programs were overlapping, with redundancies and duplication. Across them, there was collected evidence of success in certain targeted areas, such as for dislocated workers. This near cacophony of federal job training programs was tamed a bit with the Personal Responsibility and Work Opportunity Reconciliation Act and the Workforce Investment Act in 1996 and 1998, respectively. In the same way as TANF was established through the former law to provide more flexibility and discretion to state and local governments, the latter accomplished the same in the area of workforce development (Cove 2017).

Education Programs

The federal government has supported education programs across levels of education to lift up and give tools to push out of poverty, starting from preschool through higher education. Among these programs are Head Start, HighScope/Perry Preschool, and education credits and tuition deductions built into the tax code.

According to the Office of Head Start in the U.S. Department of Health and Human Services (2017): "Head Start was designed to help break the cycle of poverty, providing preschool children of low-income families with a comprehensive program to meet their emotional, social, health, nutritional and psychological needs. A key tenet of the program established that it be culturally responsive to the communities served, and that the communities have an investment in its success through the contribution of volunteer hours and other donations as nonfederal share." The evaluation of Head Start impact is mixed, with some showing gains for participating children during the preschool years but disappearing after high school. More recent research suggests early life lessons may become apparent again in later life, and so the lost gains reappear. Despite the mixed findings, Head Start remains the longest running anti-poverty program established as part of Johnson's War on Poverty. It is a popular program that has potential to at least ensure children born to poverty have a fighting chance to promote out of this lifestyle.

Another preschool program is HighScope, which presents a very specific curriculum for preschool education. HighScope officials conducted a longitudinal study following children through age forty, showing strong positive results. HighScope (2017) summarizes the research and findings:

> This study—perhaps the most well-known of all HighScope research efforts—examines the lives of 123 children born in poverty and at high risk of failing in school.

From 1962–1967, at ages 3 and 4, the subjects were randomly divided into a program group that entered a high-quality preschool program based on High-Scope's participatory learning approach, and a comparison group who received no preschool program. Published in Lifetime Effects, the study's most recent phase—HighScope Perry Preschool Study Through Age 40 [2005]—interviewed 97% of the study participants still living at the age of 40. Additional data was gathered from the subjects' school, social services, and arrest records.

The study found that adults at age 40 who underwent the preschool program had higher earnings, committed fewer crimes; were more likely to hold a job, and were more likely to have graduated from high school than adults who did not have a preschool education.

An assumption of these preschool programs is that participants will grow up more likely to attend college or pursue other higher education. This is where programs like the American Opportunity credit and Lifetime Learning credit can be helpful. These are benefits built into the tax code for individuals across income levels to claim, making access to higher levels of learning more affordable. Unlike federal grants for education, which are also available on a need or merit basis, these credits require up front payment by the individual of tuition costs. This might make them out of reach for individuals who lack discretionary cash flow.

Volunteer Programs

There are additional programs that are supported by the federal government that support similar missions as those discussed in the preceding pages. For a more complete review of some of these programs, see Bryer (2015). They include City Year, a program that places full time volunteers inside schools within low-income communities. These volunteers provide mentoring and other support to children who are academically at risk; they are supported through government funds and private/corporate sponsorship. Volunteerism is also embedded within the Head Start model, and within numerous other programs and support services. We will say more about this in describing Volunteers in Service to America in the next section. Suffice for now to say that volunteerism has been a consistent strategy to fight poverty, sometimes as a component of a larger program and sometimes as a stand-alone program.

Place-Based Promotion Policies and Programs

Programs and policies listed here are targeted to neighborhoods and communities, typically with a high percentage of individuals and families living in poverty or with other indicators of economic distress, such as high unemployment rate. Unlike the programs and policies outlined in the previous categories, these have a clear objective to not only help individuals but to provide sustainable conditions for economic development, social cohesion, and job growth. Programs and policies include:

- Hope VI Mixed-Income Communities (Choice Neighborhoods Initiative)*
- Neighborhood Revitalization Initiative (Harlem Children's Zone)
- Area Redevelopment Act
- Appalachian Regional Development Act
- Volunteers in Service to America (VISTA)*
- Community Action Program (CAP)*

HOPE VI Mixed-Income Communities (Choice Neighborhoods Initiative)
HOPE VI enables a suite of programs to assist communities with severely distressed housing to rebuild, reform, and transform. Core elements of Hope VI programming include (United States Department of Housing and Urban Development 2017):

- Changing the physical shape of public housing
- Establishing positive incentives for resident self-sufficiency and comprehensive services that empower residents
- Lessening concentrations of poverty by placing public housing in non-poverty neighborhoods and promoting mixed-income communities
- Forging partnerships with other agencies, local governments, nonprofit organizations, and private businesses to leverage support and resources

Among the plethora of programs linked to HOPE VI funding is the Choice Neighborhoods program. The program bridges sectors and leverages disparate resources to transform whole communities and the lives of people living within. The United States Department of Housing and Urban Development describes the program fully:

The Choice Neighborhoods program supports locally driven strategies to address struggling neighborhoods with distressed public or HUD-assisted housing through a comprehensive approach to neighborhood transformation. Local leaders, residents, and stakeholders, such as public housing authorities, cities, schools, police, business owners, nonprofits, and private developers, come together to create and implement a plan that transforms distressed HUD housing and addresses the challenges in the surrounding neighborhood. The program is designed to catalyze critical improvements in neighborhood assets, including vacant property, housing, services and schools.

Choice Neighborhoods is focused on three core goals:

1. Housing: Replace distressed public and assisted housing with high-quality mixed-income housing that is well-managed and responsive to the needs of the surrounding neighborhood;
2. People: Improve educational outcomes and intergenerational mobility for youth with services and supports delivered directly to youth and their families; and
3. Neighborhood: Create the conditions necessary for public and private reinvestment in distressed neighborhoods to offer the kinds of amenities and assets, including safety, good schools, and commercial activity, that are important to families' choices about their community.

To achieve these core goals, communities must develop a comprehensive neighborhood revitalization strategy, or Transformation Plan. This Transformation Plan will become the guiding document for the revitalization of the public and/or assisted housing units, while simultaneously directing the transformation of the surrounding neighborhood and positive outcomes for families. To successfully implement the Transformation Plan, applicants will need to work with public and private agencies, organizations (including philanthropic organizations), and individuals to gather and leverage resources needed to support the financial sustainability of the plan. These efforts should build community support for and involvement in the development of the plan. Implementation Grants support those communities that have undergone a comprehensive local planning process and are ready to implement their "Transformation Plan" to redevelop the neighborhood.

The Urban Institute conducted an evaluation of HOPE VI programs after ten years of operations, from 1992 to 2002. The authors conclude that evaluation was exceedingly difficult, as there was not a uniform approach and no single program to evaluate across contexts. The very flexibility that made it attractive to respond to poverty in specific communities makes it difficult to assess. They summarize (Popkin, Katz, Cunningham, Brown, Gustafson, and Turner 2004, 3):

Some people characterize it as a dramatic success, while others view it as a profound failure. There is no question that the program has had some notable accomplishments. Hundreds of profoundly distressed developments have been targeted for demolition, and many of them are now replaced with well-designed, high-quality housing serving a mix of income levels. HOPE VI has been an incubator for innovations in project financing, management, and service delivery. Some projects have helped turn around conditions in the surrounding neighborhoods and have contributed to the revitalization of whole inner-city communities. However, HOPE VI implementation has also encountered significant challenges. Some HOPE VI projects have been stalled by ineffective implementation on the part of the housing authority or conflict with city government. In others, developments were simply rehabilitated or rebuilt in the same distressed communities, with little thought to innovative design, effective services, or neighborhood revitalization.

Most troubling, for the authors of the report, and for us, with our framework focused equally on subsistence poverty and agency and status poverty, is a finding that the poor themselves had limited role in defining the character of the redeveloped communities. They summarize (Popkin et al. 2004, 3, italics added):

> Most seriously, there is substantial evidence that the original residents of HOPE VI projects have not always benefited from redevelopment, even in some sites that were otherwise successful. *This can be partly attributed to a lack of meaningful resident participation in planning and insufficient attention to relocation strategies and services.* As a consequence, some of the original residents of these developments may live in equally or even more precarious circumstances today.

This may be particularly concerning for place-based programs that more than person-centered programs rely on cooperation and inclusion of the vast array of stakeholders in that place. Despite this, the intent has been and continues to be an effort that focuses on providing opportunity, hope as it were, by transforming entire neighborhoods and lives, not seeking to protect the life of a single person or family.

Neighborhood Revitalization Initiative (Harlem Children's Zone)

Choice Neighborhoods is part of a set of place-based programs that were initiated and assessed throughout the Obama administration. Others include Promise Neighborhoods, Byrne Criminal Justice Innovation, Community Health Centers, and Behavioral Health Services. These are part of a family of programs collectively identified as the Neighborhood Revitalization Initiative (NRI). According to the Obama administration, the NRI "is operating under a shared theory of change—that an integrated, coordinated effort to increase the quality of a neighborhood's (1) educational and developmental,

(2) commercial, (3) recreational, (4) physical, and (5) social assets, sustained by local leadership over an extended period, will improve resident well-being and community quality of life" (White House Neighborhood Revitalization Initiative 2009, 2).

The approach is designed to be (ibid.):

- *Interdisciplinary*, to address the interconnected problems in distressed neighborhoods;
- *Coordinated*, to align the requirements of federal programs so that local communities can more readily braid together different funding streams;
- *Place-based*, to leverage investments by geographically targeting resources and drawing on the compounding effect of well-coordinated action;
- *Data- and results-driven*, to facilitate program monitoring and evaluation, to guide action needed to make adjustments in policy or programming, and to learn what works and develop best practices; and
- *Flexible*, to adapt to changing conditions on the ground.

One of the programs of the NRI, in addition to Choice Neighborhoods, is Promise Neighborhoods. Whereas Choice Neighborhoods is spearheaded by the United States Department of Housing and Urban Development, Promise Neighborhoods is spearheaded by the United States Department of Education. It is described as such (ibid., 3):

> Inspired by experiences of initiatives such as the Harlem Children's Zone, Promise Neighborhoods supports projects that are designed to create a comprehensive continuum of education programs and family and community supports, with great schools at the center, that will significantly improve the educational and developmental outcomes of children and youth, from birth through college and career, in the nation's most distressed communities.

The inspiration for Promise Neighborhoods, as stated, was the Harlem Children's Zone (HCZ). "Our goal is simple—to give our kids the individualized support they need to get to and through college and become productive, self-sustaining adults. Realizing this goal is difficult and complex, particularly since we are working with over 12,000 youth, many of them with tough challenges" (Harlem Children's Zone 2017).

The pipeline runs across age brackets from birth through college and implements integrated services that leverage resources and partnerships from multiple agencies to assist both the target youth population and their whole family. HCZ reports positive results in college readiness and completion, family stability, and overall social and academic success due to its array of programs. As such, the program has support from the highest levels, including President Barack Obama: "An all-encompassing, all-hands-on-deck, anti-poverty effort that is literally saving a generation of children" (Harlem Children's Zone 2017b).

Area Redevelopment Act and Appalachian Regional Development Act

The Area Redevelopment Act and Appalachian Regional Development Act reflect initiatives of the Kennedy and Johnson administrations, respectively, to invest federal resources in targeted areas and most particularly rural depressed areas. James Sundquist, who served as deputy undersecretary of agriculture for President Johnson, defines the rural poor as an afterthought within the context of these programs (Gillette 2010, 119–20):

> Now formally, of course, the Kennedy and Johnson administrations both supported rural development in the Area Redevelopment Act and the Public Works and Economic Development Act and the Appalachia Regional Development Act and in a number of the Agriculture Department measures. But these tended to be looked on by the group that might be called "urban fundamentalists" as gestures, not as serious efforts to stabilize the location of population and deal with poverty where it existed.

The programs were intended to leverage federal, state, and private resources to build the economies of local areas. These were the predecessor programs to other place-based initiatives that really took hold and took off during the Obama administration. Unlike the Obama initiatives, these involved heavier federal investment. Focusing on rural specifically might have been politically attractive, but technically, from a cost-benefit analysis, it was perhaps risky and counter to cultural assumptions. As Sundquist tells us: "The rural areas are looked on as backwaters. The people who live there are looked on as unenterprising and hardly worth saving, because if they had any gumption, they'd get up and leave" (Gillette 2010, 120). This conflict between urban and rural intervention certainly remained constant within the framework of other War on Poverty programs, including Volunteers in Service to America and the Community Action Program.

Volunteers in Service to America (VISTA)

VISTA was officially created as part of the Economic Opportunity Act of 1964 as a domestic Peace Corps designed to place Americans into impoverished communities as volunteers for one year, in the same manner Peace Corps places volunteers in developing countries for two years. The idea of having a place-based volunteer program domestically within the United States, and the identity of the program, was difficult to establish in the early years. One Johnson administration official describes the situation (Gillette 2010, 289):

> Nobody knew who the hell we were. And the Peace Corps had all this glamour about foreign countries and being a help to some poor African in some far-off, exotic place. Who the hell wanted to help some poor Africans, third-, fifth-generation residents of Harlem? But that changed.

The choice of urban or rural settings presented a conflict in the early years of VISTA. As another Johnson administration official recalls: "The success of the VISTA volunteers in major urban programs always got hung up on the fact that the people who lived in an urban ghetto, for example, were much, much less receptive to some college graduate from white suburbia coming into Harlem to run a nursery education program than a Bolivian farmer might be to the same kind of individual going to live in a village in Bolivia [through the Peace Corps]" (Gillette 2010, 290). The benefit of this kind of program, then, was not only to benefit communities but to help educate the people who, effectively, are the existing or emergent elite members of society about poverty and the look and feel of the impoverished throughout the country. The same administration official describes the objective (Gillette 2010, 290):

> One of the thoughts in VISTA, of course, was that there would be a benefit in taking college graduates and some technically qualified people and giving them assignments which would give them experience they otherwise probably would not have—working on an Indian reservation, or working in a poor Appalachian community, or working in an urban ghetto area—and that this kind of cross-fertilization between different areas of the country, different parts of the country, not only in terms of geography but in terms of rural-urban and the types of social areas of the country that we have, was a major benefit, and that understanding the patchwork-quilt nature of the country and what goes on inside of some of the other pieces of the quilt that we live in is important for all Americans in exactly the same way that it's important for all Americans to understand Bolivians and Ethiopians and Pakistanis better.

VISTA has persisted for more than fifty years, though not without controversy or continual threats to its funding. During the Clinton administration, it was embedded within the AmeriCorps umbrella and housed officially within the Corporation for National and Community Service—an agency that is on the target list for potential elimination by the Trump administration. Part of the controversy was and remains that VISTA volunteers are not simply passive onlookers trying to help develop programs that might assist people survive their poverty or places to grow out of impoverished conditions. They are, as one Johnson administration official tells it, "agents of change" (Gillette 2010, 292).

> It didn't take the VISTA volunteer a hell of a long time, whether he was in Harlem or in the South Side of Chicago or in Appalachia or in a Navajo reservation. In the latter, for example, it didn't take him long to figure out that if the white people have got a municipal water system, and the Indians have got to travel in the same county five miles to get enough water in a bunch of five-gallon cans, then there's something the matter with the public system, and if you're there to do something about poverty, you begin showing up at the water authority meetings, and you say things that they really don't want to hear.

A further example of teaching little kids to read is interesting, insofar as this is precisely the kind of program that is found in VISTA projects that are initiated in the 21st century. One such example comes from the university home of the authors: University of Central Florida. Here the Center for Public and Nonprofit Management in the School of Public Administration implemented a VISTA project focused on academic success of homeless youth. VISTA volunteers were recruited and placed in schools, school district offices, nonprofit homeless serving organizations including shelters, and faith organizations; the aim was to develop new programs and initiatives to help homeless youth succeed despite their homeless situation, and to help parents of these youth understand their rights under other federal laws (Bryer, Augustin, and Bachman 2015).

Community Action Program (CAP)

We have discussed the CAP and Community Action agencies already within this text; here we unpack it more. Fundamentally, CAP was designed to place decision-making about poverty programs and initiatives at the most local level and to specifically include participation of the poor in that process—Maximum Feasible Participation of the poor. The intent was not necessarily to cooperate with local authorities from municipal governments, but neither was it necessarily to stand as adversaries to the existing power structures. Yet, the program was implemented in more this adversarial form (Melish 2010), which favored a "more radical agenda of arousing the poor"

(Gillette 2010, 81; Moynihan 1969). The guiding intent of the program designers, though, was not conflict but empowerment.

The director of the Office of Economic Opportunity (OEO), Sargent Shriver, recalls the question of empowerment in parallel to how he considered the same question in running the Peace Corps (Gillette 2010, 81):

> [D]oing community development in Ecuador is, philosophically and substantially, no different than doing the same thing in some West Virginia hollow. Now, I'm not trying to say West Virginia Hollows are like Ecuador, but the concept of going to Ecuador to try to help people decide their own problems, and to energize them, motivate them, assist them to be able to handle their own problems themselves, is no different than the psychology you take into West Virginia or to the South Bronx. In the Peace Corps, one called this process 'community development'; in the war against poverty, we called it "community action."

Community action was designed to provide discretion and flexibility to individuals at the local level; they could establish their system and structure, the kind of relationships between municipal government, nonprofit organizations, and citizens, and the kinds of programs they would develop and for which they would seek funding. This meant that community action, as implemented, varied greatly when looking at diverse urban areas and between urban and rural areas.

Community Action Agencies, still in operation in 2017, provide an array of services, including: coordination of services; facilitation of citizen participation; emergency assistance for food, shelter, and energy; youth mentoring; adult education; food banks; Meals on Wheels for homebound elderly; day care; family counseling; job training; financial literacy; transportation assistance; homeownership assistance; housing weatherization; business planning and loan facilitation; and, health clinics. Individual services are determined by local agencies that have participation from government and nonprofit sectors, at a minimum, and involvement from the poor directly.

Community action is funded through a mix of sources, including from federal government block grants. These grants include the Community Service Block Grant (CSBG) and Community Development Block Grant (CDBG). Both have been threatened with elimination or substantive cutback. In the next chapter, we dig deeper into CDBG as a case study of a poverty program at risk.

CHAPTER SIX

~

Case Study of Community Development Block Grant Program

The Community Development Block Grant (CDBG) aims to provide financial support to communities in order to address a wide range of community development needs, such as affordable housing, suitable living environment, and job opportunities for low and moderate income people. The program aims to ensure that the grantee develops a plan for civic engagement of low-income families in solving community issues by, for instance, providing access to local public meetings, opportunities to review proposed programs and write complaints (United States Department of Housing and Urban Development 2017).

President Trump's 2018 budget blueprint targets the CDBG for elimination. According to the Office of Management and Budget, "the program is not well-targeted to the poorest populations and has not demonstrated results. The Budget devolves community and economic development activities to the State and local level and redirects federal resources to other activities" (United States Office of Management and Budget 2017, 25). Critics of this elimination proposal suggest such an action can lead to irreversible issues and increase the level of poverty.

This chapter addresses the following questions: What are successes and failures of the CDBG in addressing poverty in the United States? What is the governance theory and structure supporting CDBG?

We focus on this policy as a case example given its potential impact on all three forms of poverty: subsistence, agency, and status. It is also a program with a relatively long history and with potential engagement not just across levels of government but across sectors as well. Given its robustness and complexity, it is an ideal program for separate analysis.

Theoretical Lens for Understanding CDBG Governance Design and Implementation

CDBG is a policy that aims to distribute power and resources to local governments and communities. Through mutual adjustment, deliberative processes, and horizontal relations, the grant allows low and medium income citizens to manage social issues, such as lack of affordable housing, employment opportunities, and access to goods and services, which cause poverty in their communities and prevent fulfillment of their human potential (Skidelsky and Skidelsky 2012).

The policy, looking in from the outside, is based on an assumption of conflict within communities. Conflict emerges through individual and intergroup interactions, which are guided by self-interests, which themselves are not aligned. These interactions, however, are a necessary component of social life in order for individuals to achieve independent and group identities (Follett 1918). Conflict, then, is inevitable (Fry 1989).

Conflict theory assumes that societies experience unequal distribution of resources, which eventually lead to conflicting interests between those who possess power and control resources and those who do not (Turner and Turner 1998). There are two potential processes that can help communities resolve conflicts grounded in disparate resource-based interests: centralism and mutual adjustment (Lindblom 1990).

Mutual adjustment is "a process of crystallization of different norms and frameworks which takes place through a series of exchanges between people placed in different structural positions" (Eisenstadt 1965, 22). It is a mechanism of social problem solving or betterment of social issues through the state or other social processes. As such, it is a process that stands in distinction to centralism, which does not allow for full inclusion of diverse stakeholders; conflicts are not resolved when decisions are centrally controlled.

Figure 6.1 summarizes this conceptual framework. Centralism illustrates policies enacted by the ruling class, which lead to social inequality and poverty. However, according to the literature, mutual adjustment can contribute to equal distribution of goods and services to citizens. Thus, we suggest that social policies, that aim to provide mutual adjustment in the form of equal distribution of resources, access to public goods and services, and power for

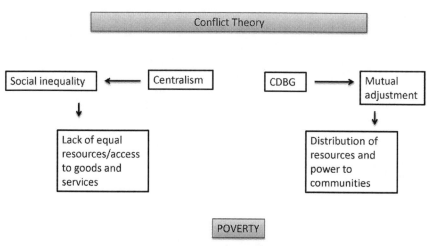

Figure 6.1. Framework for Analyzing Community Development Block Grant Program

decision-making process among citizens, can eventually lead to decreases in poverty in all of its forms.

History of CDBG

The Housing and Community Development Act created the CDBG in 1974. Poverty is one of the main targets of CDBG. However, the program addresses multiple dimensions of community need, which together contribute to improvement of communities' well-being and a decrease of poverty.

The primary goal of CDBG is the development of viable and vital urban communities (Sinkienė, Gaulė, Bruneckienė, Zaleckis, Bryer, and Ramanauskas 2017); the goal is pursued by providing low and moderate-income (LMI) communities with affordable housing, expanding economic and employment opportunities, creation of suitable living environments, preventing and eliminating slums, and addressing urgent issues that pose immediate threats to communities' health and well-being.

Core principles of CDBG include (United States Department of Housing and Urban Development 2016):

- benefit low and moderate income individuals
- flexible use of funds, local decision-making
- community participation (hearings, program performance review, complaints submission)

- networking, building partnerships, leveraging funds from other sources
- strategic investments

Funds are allocated across states according to poverty level, population, percentage of housing stock that is pre-1940, population growth rate and overcrowding (United States Government Accountability Office 2016; Dreier et al. 2014). In order to get a grant, a community or area within the community must meet a 51 percent threshold for LMI families. Seventy percent of federal funds are distributed among entitled communities; 30 percent of funds are channeled through states to non-entitlement communities. The Government Accountability Office (2016) defines entitlement communities as "principal cities of metropolitan statistical areas, other metropolitan cities with populations of at least 50,000, and qualified urban counties with populations of 200,000 or more (excluding the populations of entitlement cities)" (GAO 2016, 3).

Practices of CDBG

Citizen participation is a key element of the CDBG program. Impoverished and moderate income citizens are given the opportunity to attend public hearings, review activities proposed for CDBG projects, and provide input by participating in decision-making processes regarding budget allocation. Another requirement of CDBG is to meet the needs of non-English speaking residents, who are expected to take part in public hearings. Procedurally, these processes align with ideas embedded within the theory of mutual adjustment.

As of 2013, 9.8 million people benefitted from public service activities, and 3.3 million people benefitted from financed public improvements. Low and moderate-income families got access to new community clinics, libraries, community centers, and thousands of rehabilitated homes. Also, CDBG funds were used to improve drinking water systems and reconstruct roads (United States Department of Housing and Urban Development 2017).

CDBG projects are designed to serve the entire poor community or a smaller area within the community. Also, the program serves particular clientele, such as centers for seniors or homeless people, or projects, that can directly benefit LMI individuals. Thus, the program addresses the issues and needs common to the overall community, as well as individual needs. For example, CDBG can allocate funds for restoration of single-family housing, or create job opportunities that will be occupied by LMI people (United States Government Accountability Office 2016).

Challenges of CDBG

CDBG has shown a great number of successful examples in addressing poverty and revitalizing communities, through allocating flexible funding and allowing citizens to make decisions on fund expenditures. However, the program has some substantial shortcomings.

First, the sources of data on community income and poverty level are limited. According to the GAO (2016) analysis, it is very difficult to identify the appropriate threshold for defining poverty by using income measures in order to allocate funds. "The distribution of grant funding per person in poverty in cities was not consistently aligned with overall poverty rates" (United States Government Accountability Office 2012, 4). The majority of cities, except for the cities with the highest poverty rates, received the same amount of funding per poor person. However, CDBG does not take into account the severity of life conditions of the poor. Furthermore, GAO reports that some cities with a higher unemployment rate receive less funding than some cities with lower unemployment rates (United States Government Accountability Office 2012).

Before the year 2000, HUD was using the U.S. Census Bureau decennial census long form in order to identify income level. In 2005 the Census Bureau replaced decennial census with an annual American Community Survey (ACS), which became the basis for gathering data on LMI level in communities. The ACS uses a smaller sample size than Decennial Census Long Form, which increases the sampling errors (United States Government Accountability Office 2016). However, small designated and rural areas, and non-entitlement communities are still allowed to use the 2000 Decennial Census Long Form, because decennial census splits areas by county subdivision, rural and urban areas, which give more chances to reach out the population in non-entitlement communities (see table 6.1). However, GAO (2016) reports that stakeholders refer to fluctuations in an individual's or community's income over a year as the main challenge, associated with measuring income and poverty rates in neighborhoods.

Second, CDBG allows local governments and communities flexibility to select activities that receive funding. Rosenfeld et al. (1995) find that "fiscally healthy cities are more likely to fund housing programs because they lack areas with concentrated poverty. Conversely, poorer cities have higher public works expenditures because they can identify areas that meet program guidelines for areal benefits" (1995, 70). The authors also claim that the funding decisions are not always dictated by the fiscal health of the communities but by political characteristics. Horizontally reformed cities put a

Table 6.1. Selected Differences Between 2000 Decennial Census Long Form and the American Community Survey Before and After 2011

	2000 Decennial Census Long Form	*American Community Survey (before 2011)*	*American Community Survey (starting June 2011)*
Sample sizes	20.9 million housing unit addresses (roughly 17.1 percent of all addresses)	2.9 million housing unit addresses annually, or 14.5 million for the 5-year estimates (5-year sample is 12.5 percent of housing unit addresses)	3.54 million housing unit addresses annually, or 17.7 million addresses for the 5-year estimate (5-year sample is 13 percent of all addresses)
Frequency of data collection	Once every 10 years – all surveys were completed within a few months of April 1 during the year of the survey	Ongoing	Ongoing
Smallest geographic level of available data for low- and moderate-income summary data	Split-block group	Block group	Block group

Note. Source: GAO-16-734 Community Development Block Grants

greater emphasis on economic development, while unreformed bureaucratic governments focus more on social services (Rosenfeld et al. 1995).

This raises the third and the most important challenge: inability to monitor project efficiency and performance, as well as determine the end user of funds. First, grants are allocated to the address of the primary grant recipient, and that does not allow monitors to determine the exact location where the grant is spent. Second, since the grants are distributed to geographic areas, it creates an issue in determining the recipient of funds (United States Government Accountability Office 2012). This situation creates a challenge to identify the outcomes of grant programs and their efficiency in improving communities' well-being and decreasing poverty rates.

The analysis shows, that although the development block grant has proven its ability to enhance community well-being, by providing affordable housing, creating job opportunities, giving access to healthcare and social services to poor and moderate-income communities, there are challenges such as lack of tools to measure the exact poverty rates, monitor allocation of funds, and measure the outcomes of grant projects. However, these challenges only indicate questions regarding the efficiency and effectiveness of CDBG; such a critique does not provide any data that indicate inefficiency of the program as has been suggested by members of the Trump administration.

Political Challenges to
CDBG and Other Anti-Poverty Programs

In the 2018 "Budget Blueprint to Make American Great Again," the Trump administration recommends elimination of the CDBG, stating its inefficiency to target poor populations and improve the well-being of communities. However, the Office of Management and Budget has not provided any evidence of the programs' overall ineffectiveness or inefficiency, nor do they consider potentially enhanced community relations that would be expected given emphases on mutual adjustment practices to resolve conflict.

This kind of recommendation is indicative of other recommendations found within the budget blueprint, expressed by members of Congress, and heard by interest groups throughout the country in 2017. Given the political dynamic, we stand at a moment when the manner in which goods and services, support and guidance, are provided to the poor can be fundamentally transformed.

We can trace the fundamental transformation that may occur now to the Reagan administration, when, in 1988, President Reagan declared: "Some years ago, the Federal government declared war on poverty, and poverty won." Such judgments, grounded in data showing limited impact, or lack of data showing positive impact, and grounded in biases against and perceptions of the poor as included-out citizens, enable policy windows to open and transformations to occur.

To contextualize the Trump administration's recommendation to eliminate CDBG, we briefly review related recommendations from the White House and Congress. The kinds of plans being discussed by the Trump administration are captured by news headlines:

- Trump to propose big cuts to safety-net in new budget, slashing Medicaid and opening door to other limits (the *Washington Post*, May 21, 2017)

- Trump's plans to cut food stamps could hit his supporters hardest (the *Washington Post*, May 22, 2017)
- America's safety net is at risk from Trump's budget ax (CNN Money, May 22, 2017)
- Can religious charities take the place of the welfare state? Supporters of Trump's budget are eager to restore the central role of faith-based organizations in serving the poor—but it's not clear they can be an adequate substitute for government (*The Atlantic*, March 26, 2017)
- Trump's plan to cut national service programs breaks decades of tradition (the *New York Times*, May 26, 2017)
- Comments on poverty start uproar (the *New York Times*, May 26, 2017)

These are news outlets that perhaps are not considered to be favorable to the Trump administration. They are peddlers of "fake news," according to oft-repeated claims by the president and his surrogates. Nevertheless, the headlines reflect the stark shift that may be coming if the president gets even a little of what he and his team want.

The Trump administration early in its tenure has adopted a strategy of threatening funding cuts for or outright elimination of numerous programs that have been created over the past fifty years to fight poverty. The strategy is grounded in a desire for evidence-based policymaking but is also ideological, representing a view that a smaller government is best and personal responsibility should be primary in considering social supports. As such, programs that have been threatened with cuts or elimination include those that have been championed by politicians of both parties over the years.

For example, national service programs embedded within the Corporation for National and Community Service (CNCS) have been threatened. These programs include AmeriCorps, Senior Corps, and the program that started it all, VISTA—Volunteers in Service to America (Green 2017). It is not wholly unusual for these programs to be threatened; it happens with some regularity every budget cycle, but until the Trump administration, presidents of both parties have been supportive of subsidized volunteer initiatives. Indeed, under previous presidents, national service programs have been expanded, including under presidents George H. W. Bush, William Clinton, George W. Bush, and Barack Obama. Like CDBG, national service programs have not always passed muster in terms of demonstrated impact, but the evidence base is growing (Bryer 2015). Nonetheless, under Trump's plan, national service and volunteer initiatives would return responsibility to the private and nonprofit sectors—both of which are existing partners whose resources are leveraged in national service programs.

The administration is also reportedly considering changes to the waivers permitted under SNAP to states and localities based on the unemployment rate. State and local governments can now apply for a waiver to the requirement that able-bodied SNAP beneficiaries work. The waiver is possible where the unemployment rate in a particular area is too high and job prospects too limited to realistically allow all able-bodied adults to find employment. Changes to the waiver policy would demonstrate a commitment to work, not welfare, but the real world impact could be significant in providing access to meals (Dewey and Jan 2017).

Suggested changes to SNAP and other programs are partially a response to the upswing in use of these programs and easing of requirements for eligibility enacted during the Obama administration as a response to the recession. Administration officials consider the job market sufficiently recovered that a return to previous requirements and even strengthening of requirements to receive benefits are in order. Proponents of existing programs and programmatic rules argue that these safety-net programs prevent a full slide to deep poverty and are not enough for survival without working in some way (Paletta 2017), and with respect to SNAP, only 14 percent of the beneficiary population are considered able-bodied and not working (Dewey and Jan 2017)—a figure that can certainly be lower, but, ask opponents to Trump administration ideas, at what cost to those who are following the rules and trying to work.

Capping or reversing Medicaid expansion, possibly as part of an overhaul (repeal and replace) of the Affordable Care Act, also would change the ways in which support is granted to citizens. Potential proposals under debate during the summer of 2017 would change the funding formula for Medicaid, providing potentially either a block grant to states for flexible use, and reducing the overall federal contribution, or a fixed amount per Medicaid enrollee, again reducing overall federal contribution. The number of people covered by Medicaid would potentially be reduced, and individual states would experiment with variations in eligibility requirements, including work and time limit requirements (Luhby 2017). There is still a long way to go before and if there is any major or minor reform to the Affordable Care Act; at the time of this writing the U.S. Senate in dramatic fashion has failed to pass a bill that would move in that direction.

Suffice to say, however, that Republican plans would shift away from an individual mandate to purchase health insurance towards individual choice—a move critics suggest would lead to a vast increase in the number of uninsured Americans, a reduction in the percentage of insured who are healthy and not in need of expensive healthcare, and thus an overall increase in premiums for those left in the market. Proponents counter that they would encourage enrolling through a variety of mechanisms, including through associations and membership organizations that would form larger negotiating blocks with drug companies and medical providers to keep costs down. This is all speculation, but the debate is real, dynamic, and the outcome can be incremental change to existing law or substantial change that would force a new reality on particularly needy people who need assistance accessing affordable healthcare.

The same philosophy undergirds the administration's position regarding CDBG, and the critics of cutting funding align as expected: to cut the program will eliminate a vital lifeline for the most needy among us. A popular rallying point for critics of the plan to eliminate CDBG has been and will continue to be Meals on Wheels. This is a program, operated in partnership with nonprofit organizations and with substantial volunteer support, which provides fresh meals to homebound elderly. The administration has argued that there is no evidence that the program actually works or is cost-effective.

Overall, the administration is guided by an ideology oriented towards small government and personal responsibility, linked to a technocratic belief in evidence-based policymaking. The same are reflected in a report of the United States House of Representatives Republican Conference Task Force on Poverty, Opportunity, and Upward Mobility (2016). Agree or disagree with the policy prescriptions, they represent a viewpoint that will be included in any future policymaking.

Future of CDBG

CDBG represents a policy that allows for Lindblom's (1990) "mutual adjustment" by promoting public participation of poor and moderate income families, and integration of citizens' interests through addressing common needs in communities. However, mutual adjustment disperses authority, bringing extreme fragmentation in communities (Lindblom 1990). This fragmentation is manifested through conflicts between the included-out and included-in citizens.

According to conflict theory, the domination of elitist powers leads to social inequalities, lack of equal distribution of resources, and access to public goods and services, which are the causes of poverty. While decentralizing power and distributing flexible funds to the community level, the government shifts federal centralism to a local or community level centralism. The public choice becomes more elitist than egalitarian. According to Smith and Larimer (2013), citizens who actively participate in decision-making processes are only a small minority who do not necessarily represent preferences of others. Citizen activists at the community level form an elite minority group (Smith and Larimer 2013), and those whom they claim to represent often lack the capacity to hold their "representatives" to account (Montanaro 2012).

For example, mayors and governors have criticized CDBG on the basis that funding is sometimes spent on community pet projects "rather than helping poor neighborhoods" (Dreier 2014, 150). Goldfield (1993) suggests that most of the funds are allocated to the marginal areas where local politicians could get quick results. For example, in Memphis, although the money went to black neighborhoods, these neighborhoods were of "moderate income with a relatively high proportion of homeownership" (Goldfield, in Hirsch and Mohl 1993, 167). This example suggests that centralist power is being formed at the local and community level, bringing a lack of representative decisions.

Although CDBG provides flexible funds to local communities, it failed to monitor the way funds are spent. Both bureaucratic expertise, or centralism and political accountability, or mutual adjustment are necessary for addressing social and economic issues at all levels of government (Farazmand 2010). Mutual adjustment allows for democratic processes and citizen participation in decision-making processes in addressing community needs. Centralism and bureaucratic accountability can help with monitoring efficiency of grant projects, evaluating performance and ensuring that targets of the impoverished population are reached. Better information on program outcomes will help determine whether or not CBDG leads to efficient, effective, and representative short and long-term results.

Toward War on Poverty and Impoverished Citizenship for the 21st Century

In this chapter, we have examined the CDBG and how it addresses poverty in communities. In the past forty years, CDBG has achieved significant results in helping low and moderate-income people and revitalizing communities. Although the Trump administration recommends elimination of CDBG, we suggest that the program can remain and that it can be a core component of the War on Poverty and Impoverished Citizenship in the 21st century. The challenges we identify in this brief case analysis, along with challenges identified in preceding chapters related to measurement and treatment of poverty in all its forms, and empowerment of the poor and the poor's representatives, provide the launch pad for specifying an agenda to renew the war and, this time, to win it.

∽

CHAPTER SEVEN

War on Poverty and Impoverished Citizenship for the 21st Century

The war on the poor, the war on citizenship, the war on poverty, and the war for skepticism will be fought on the following fronts: (1) expertise versus mass competence, (2) transparency versus informed judgment, (3) volunteers versus active citizens with the state, (4) consumerism versus citizenship, (5) quantity versus quality, (6) representation versus inclusivity, and (7) tolerance of ignorance through manipulation versus empowerment. We summarize these battlefronts and then present a unifying framework indicating the path forward. The goal is to move poor and non-poor citizens both from included-out status politically and ethically, and culturally and religiously, by targeting agency and status poverty. We close this chapter with further discussion of possible reforms regarding legal citizenship and reducing barriers for the poor to be included-in here as well.

Expertise Versus Mass Competence

I engage my students studying democracy in an exercise. I propose to them that citizens need to demonstrate basic knowledge about how government works before they can vote or participate in a meeting. The exercise is intended to shine a spotlight on the lack of political intelligence and democratic competence within the mass population. In the United States, privilege is given to professional stakeholders and government authorities in decision-making. Though opportunities are provided for citizens to provide their input, citizens are not provided education or guidance to make use of those opportunities in a way that is meaningful for themselves or their communities. To strengthen our democratic relations and the relations between government and citizen, we need a more rigorous and systematic approach to citizen education.

Applied to the poor and the idea of Maximum Feasible Participation (MFP), we might consider learning from the community organizer, Saul Alinksy (1989). His method of organizing citizens for civic action was also an educational process: he effectively manipulated citizens to help them learn the limitations of their power and the opportunities they have for enhancing their power within the community and in the eyes of government. His approach was not simply to tell citizens what they should do to secure better housing; he engaged citizens in an exercise of discovery so they actually experienced the power of their action. For example, he might in the middle of the night post eviction notices on doors of public housing residences. This was a ploy to get poor residents to realize that such short-term eviction was possible, unless they organized and developed their power. Alinsky engaged in manipulation not as a permanent condition but as a strategy towards informed empowerment.

This is one role for government: educate the people so they understand their rights and their opportunities to help create better qualities of life. Importantly, such an education process is not for government alone. Other societal institutions need to participate in this process, including media and, significantly, universities. Universities in particular can adopt the role not only of educating tuition paying students but educating members of society through research, teaching, and service partnerships (Bryer 2014).

All of this contributes to the idea of mass competence; not everyone can be an expert in all things, but most people can achieve basic competence and rationality to make their own independent and well-considered decisions (Bloom 2016). Expertise in and of itself is not a negative attribute of a civilized society, far from it. Expertise exerted at the expense of education for the masses, and particularly the most vulnerable, is problematic. Easterly (2013, 7) summarizes this point:

> The technocratic illusion is that poverty results from a shortage of expertise, whereas poverty is really about a shortage of rights. The emphasis on the problem of expertise makes the problem of rights worse. The technical problems of the poor (and the absence of technical solutions for those problems) are a *symptom* of poverty, not a *cause* of poverty.

Easterly writes in the context of development economics and global poverty, and he fears the expert-based policy designs handed to dictators will be implemented without full and proper contextualization and adaptation, and with a high possibility of corruption. We can apply the same underlying logic to developed countries, not expressing concern for any less-than beneficent tendencies of dictators but concern for technical-rational systems that prevent the poor themselves from engaging their situation and co-developing their solutions. Technical-rational systems can be just as insidious as the worst authoritarian dictator (Adams and Balfour 2014).

Nick Lyon, director of the Michigan Department of Health and Human Services, is quoted in a policy document by the United States House of Representatives Republican Party Conference's Task Force on Poverty, Opportunity, and Upward Mobility: "Instead of working with the individual and determining that person's goals, we often are more concerned with programmatic requirements, leading to an overly complex system that is difficult for all of us. . . ." (2016, 6). This is a statement about a patchwork of independently well-designed programs, grounded in theories and/or data about what works; the implication is a system that is technically impressive but without grounding in citizen or service-recipient understanding. There is, as Easterly (2013) calls it, a tyranny of expertise.

As such, the goal for an MFP program for the 21st century that battles agency and status poverty in equal measure to subsistence poverty should be driven by a quest for mass competence, not expertise.

Transparency Versus Informed Judgment

It is very popular across the globe, amongst Open Government Partnership participating nations in particular, to promote increasing transparency. Transparency is vital to mitigate corruption and to provide information to citizens so they can become active citizens.

There is a significantly negative pitfall to transparency, however, if the act of sharing information overwhelms citizens rather than engages them. For example, posting all available statistics about city operations, funding, and societal condition can be helpful for those citizens who know what they are seeking, or for professional stakeholders and academic researchers. However, open information, in the hands of someone without complete information can be dangerous.

We will give a quick example. In the State of Florida, as in other states within the United States, anyone can enter a website and find the salary information for all state employees, including university professors. However, this can be dangerous. First, the information may not be complete; in other words, the true cost of the employee might not be known as we calculate benefits besides direct salary. Second, and more important, salary information presented without further explanation about the employee's job description or performance is misleading in that citizens can make conclusions that are not accurate. For instance: "Why are we paying Professor XYZ so much money to teach two classes each semester?" When core context is missing from open sharing of data, citizens can make conclusions that lead to misunderstanding and adversarial action with government and with each other.

Another example comes from the U.S. federal government rulemaking process. Federal regulatory agencies post their proposed rules and regulations on a single, searchable web portal called regulations.gov. This openness and ease of access to information about rules and regulations is intended to make it easier for citizens and professional stakeholders alike to identify actions the government might be taking and to share their opinion about such actions. The stated objective of regulations.gov is to make regulatory decision-making both more efficient and open to public participation. However, research on the citizen input suggests the openness of information alone did not facilitate informed judgment about the issues; indeed, citizen comments were driven by emotion and incomplete information, despite having full records and background material provided (Bryer 2013).

It is for this reason that we can question the general rhetoric that often accompanies calls for increased transparency. The House of Representatives Republican Party Task Force on Poverty, Opportunity, and Upward Mobility suggests in its report (2016, 30): "Streamlining information will empower students and families with the knowledge they need to make smart college decisions . . . Existing transparency efforts at the federal level should be simplified to reduce confusion for students, and federal agencies should coordinate more effectively, avoid duplication, and deliver information in a format that is easy to understand." The substantive focus of these sentences is in regard to higher education information, essentially to enable a more informed consumer to make the best choices for their time and monetary investment. This is indeed the promise of transparency, but simplifying the presentation of information according to the agenda of the simplifier does not empower or enable truly informed judgment.

Instead, we need to consider ways to transform simple transparency or sharing of data into informed judgment. Applied to poverty, the practice fifty years ago was to inform impoverished citizens of their rights and direct them to apply for benefits. Today, we can share much data about poverty rates, welfare benefits, and so on. These data can generate sympathy or concern amongst the citizenry, or they can generate scorn between those not impoverished and those enduring the strain of poverty. The question is: how do we

share data that creates a sense of shared responsibility for alleviating poverty—its root causes and consequences? Transparency cannot just be about
sharing; it must be about educating and activating, where data and information become the glue that binds diverse citizens together in common cause.

As such, the goal for an MFP program for the 21st century that battles
agency and status poverty in equal measure to subsistence poverty should
be driven by a quest for informed judgment, not potentially overwhelming
transparency.

Volunteers Versus Active Citizens

In the United States, when presidents encourage citizens to be active, they
are more likely to encourage volunteerism as compared to active and direct
engagement with the government to help develop new policies and programs
(Bryer 2012b). This has been true over the past fifty years and across political parties. Two presidents that have taken a different perspective are Jimmy
Carter and Barack Obama. They both developed plans and policies for directly engaging citizens in rulemaking and other policy discussions.

The difference between volunteerism and active citizenship is one of
intensity of effort. The best way to think about it is this way: a volunteer
is someone who occasionally gives of his or her time to help those in need,
including those living in poverty. For instance, they volunteer time at a food
bank or homeless shelter. One step above the volunteer is someone who
actively organizes citizens for volunteerism. Rather than simply showing
up occasionally, this citizen organizes and mobilizes citizens to give of their
time. The active citizen is one who does not stop at that point; this citizen
does not just try to treat the symptoms of poverty but actively asks the question: why is there so much poverty to treat, and what can we do from a policy
level to change it?

Active citizens need not be collaborative with government; their activism
can be adversarial, within the context of electoral politics, ensconced fully
within civil society, and/or manifested through participation in "standard"
participatory processes such as public hearings and community meetings
(Cooper, Bryer, and Meek 2006). The form of activism is not as important
as the intensity; seeking good will with government leaders and encouraging blanket or blind trust refutes the need for healthy skepticism of the kind
required to challenge status quo polices, programs, and institutions.

As such, the goal for an MFP program for the 21st century that battles
agency and status poverty in equal measure to subsistence poverty should be
driven by a quest for active citizenship, not (or not only) volunteerism.

Consumerism Versus Citizenship

Impoverished citizenship is often supplanted in political discourse as well as in individual action by the image of the vibrant consumer. Consumerism can boost economies, which can potentially lift individuals out of poverty. However, it does not change the foundations that give rise to poverty and vast rates of income inequality, nor can it typically lift whole communities out of poverty. As with the volunteer, a consumer is a vital role for a citizen in an economically and socially healthy society, but it cannot replace the role of citizen (Denhardt and Denhardt 2015; Kalu 2017).

Taken at face value, a consumer role for the people living in a country or community may devalue the more active role of citizen (Denhardt and Denhardt 2015). The division in these two roles is hardly so clear in practice. Indeed, prominent governance and public administration reforms in the 1980s and 1990s were founded on the premise that government ought to treat people more like customers of private businesses. It is thought that such a role will help improve service delivery; in the same way a customer of a McDonald's demands high quality service and can register their complaint if such is not received, a "customer" of a local zoning agency or the federal Social Security Administration should have the same opportunity. With good service will come satisfied customers of government. The George W. Bush administration conflated the roles of consumer and citizens in the President's Management Agenda, calling for increased power for the citizen-customer.

We do not suggest satisfaction with government service is unimportant, but to whole scale treat the people as consumer and not as potentially active citizen, per the previous section on active citizenship, limits the responsiveness of governments to the full interests of the people rather than only to the expressed wishes or even whims of the people.

As such, the goal for an MFP program for the 21st century that battles agency and status poverty in equal measure to subsistence poverty should be driven by a quest for citizenship, not consumerism.

Quantity Versus Quality

Advocates of public participation, particularly e-participation or e-democracy, see great potential in tools and processes that can engage more people more easily. If we lower the costs of participation (Cooper 1979), we can attract more participating citizens to town hall meetings, city council meetings, and to online participation spaces. We lower costs by convening meetings at multiple times of the day and across multiple locations, providing childcare for parents, and opening a process to anyone without restriction. However, research informs us that costs of participation that are too low may lead to an increase in quantity of participation but a decrease in quality of participation (Wang and Bryer 2013). For instance, opening online discussion spaces to anyone without requiring registration or identification leads, in at least some cases, to citizen comments that are not relevant to the focus of discussion, and in which citizens do not present a credible argument in support of their position on an issue. These are the costs of democratization (Bryer 2011b).

So we must find a balance, in which costs of participation are neither too low, nor too high. We can establish requirements for participation as simple as registering a name and address to participate online or offline. Perhaps we even ask citizens to complete a short quiz to ensure they understand the basic issues to be discussed in a public meeting; this quiz would not be a barrier to entry but would enable citizens to learn a bit more about the issue and to potentially recognize their assumptions about an issue may not be accurate.

Applied to poverty, this is critical. The citizens who would be engaged—the impoverished—would be of the demographic that has traditionally not been engaged in public participation processes before. Government must then both prepare them for participation while also establishing a bar to mitigate a public process from being hijacked by citizens who were not asked to take the time to learn a little about the issues before participating. Increasingly, the online engagement is critical and can be a gateway to offline participation; ensuring an expectation of meaningful, high quality engagement is critical to transfer the same quality to the in-person environment (Butkeviciene, Bryer, Vaidelyte, and Morkevicius in press).

As such, the goal for an MFP program for the 21st century that battles agency and status poverty in equal measure to subsistence poverty should be driven by a quest for quality of participation, not (only) quantity of participation.

Representation Versus Inclusivity

In the same manner that the value of high quantity of participation is limited if not matched with meaningful, high quality participation, formal representation of citizen groups that fail to more broadly empower those groups being represented is limiting. Token participation by members of the community living in poverty on community advisory boards or other similar councils fails to develop the kinds of civic and political efficacy required to reduce the power of professional stakeholders and interest groups. Participation processes are better inclusive in their structure, so even if a small number of impoverished citizens have a position on an advisory board, they have a formal obligation to engage the community they represent.

In other words, representative roles must have rules that ensure inclusiveness and accountability of the representative; the represented must have a mechanism to understand the issues as considered by the representative; the wider array of poor and non-poor citizens must be truly empowered to self-present while having confidence in their official representatives to speak, act, or vote on their behalf.

As such, the goal for an MFP program for the 21st century that battles agency and status poverty in equal measure to subsistence poverty should be driven by a quest for inclusiveness, not representativeness.

Tolerance of Ignorance Versus Empowerment

This all wraps into the core concern: if government and citizen are on the same side, then citizens need to be empowered through engagement, education, and the development of mass competence. The status quo permits ongoing ignorance amongst citizens. If it is not seen as efficient to fully educate and develop competence of citizens, then we return to the first battlefront: expertise is privileged over competence widely distributed. Fundamentally, this is what needs to change.

It might be relatively simple to define ignorance, as the lack of information or access to information and the capacity to understand and act on information, but to define empowerment as such is more challenging. What is necessary to empower?

We have used the words "empower" or "empowerment" a couple dozen times already in these pages. We have built on the definitions of others, at least implicitly, and have defined it by exception to what it is not rather than what it is. It has been defined as a state of mind and as a fixed condition. Previously, in the first chapter we wrote: "To be sure, we are not interested in empowerment by granting political power to the masses, poor and non-poor, who can increase ability to subsist despite their ignorance. Genuine empowerment requires information and the ability to interpret the actions of others in the context of one's own self-interest."

Empowerment is a feel-good word that is used in political rhetoric, and, ironically perhaps, as a word meant to manipulate rather than, well, empower. "Empower" is used twelve times in the House Republican Task Force document referenced previously, as a condition that will arise through transparency, flexibility, and reduction in rules. The document rhetorically empowers numerous categories of people, including "Americans" (4), "states, parents, and local communities" (24), "states" (26), "young Americans" (27), "state and local community leaders" (29), "students and families" (30), "working families" (33), and "people" (34).

Empowerment ultimately means giving power where none existed, but, as we have tried to emphasize throughout this text, it requires more than being granted flexibility and information. It is more than someone with power relieving themselves of certain responsibilities and hoping the powerless take up the cause. Empowerment requires training such that it is not the absence of ignorance but the ability to use knowledge and exercise discretion. It is a "sense of personal competence, a desire for, and a willingness to take action in, the public domain" (Zimmerman and Rappaport 1988, 746). It occurs when a person has the "skills, tools, and confidence to contribute meaningfully to the social, economic, and intellectual strengthening of communities" (Bryer, Augustin, Barve, Gracia, and Perez 2013, 50).

As such, the goal for an MFP program for the 21st century that battles agency and status poverty in equal measure to subsistence poverty should be driven by a quest for empowerment, not a tolerance of ignorance.

MFP for the 21st Century

Tara Melish (2010) suggests MFP can be resurrected in better form today given advancements in theory and practice related to new governance and new accountability that rely on decentralization and collaboration integrated with performance measurement and management. At the heart of Melish's proposal is a set of values that are consistent with Ci's (2013) admonishment that agency poverty not be subjugated to subsistence poverty. Melish writes (2010, 15): "[The poor] wish to reclaim a space for themselves, to cast off notions of their 'inability' or 'dependence,' and instead compel the public and government actors to see them as human beings with dignity, agency, and a drive to be treated on the basis of equal opportunity—not charity or paternalism."

Her proposal further centers on a set of "organizational precepts and guiding principles" (2010, 11): "These include a shared policy preference for decentralization and broad stakeholder participation, flexible results-oriented policy planning, coordinated public-private partnerships, innovation and competitive experimentalism, rigorous monitoring and performance evaluation, and nationally-orchestrated incentive systems around defined performance goals and targets" (2010, 11). To achieve these aims, Melish suggests the creation of "orchestrating" bodies operating across the national landscape. One is a National Office on Poverty Alleviation, which would reside in the Executive Office of the President and serve to coordinate the various components of social welfare and anti-poverty programming. Second is a National Human Rights Commission, which would be "required to ensure that transparent monitoring processes were being independently undertaken around the nation on the impact of government policies on human rights, particularly of the most disadvantaged" (2010, 126).

These agencies will be guided by National Poverty Reduction Targets that, for instance, set a goal for reducing poverty by 50 percent over ten years. The concept here is straightforward: to draw attention to issues of poverty, there needs to be not only clearly stated goals but mechanisms for tracking movement toward goal accomplishment.

Within this context, Melish proposes "broad stakeholder responsibility and participatory commitments" that require the MFP of "all stakeholders in society, operating in increasingly broad community partnerships" (2010, 117). She continues, "such partnerships seek to take advantage of the full scope of human, financial, technological, and informational resources available, from the dense knowledge and expertise in local communities of poverty's causes, to the entrepreneurial skills, ideas, and investment potential of private business, to the civic energies of private citizens, to the research capabilities of the nation's universities and educations institutions" (117–18).

On the whole, these are sound recommendations, but they fall short on two major counts: (1) they ignore Ci's (2013) conception of agency poverty and focus on subsistence poverty, and (2) related, in focusing MFP on a broad class of stakeholders, they do not provide sufficient attention on the individual in poverty and his or her need for agency renewal and self-empowerment. As Ci argues, there must be a "severing of any links that happen to exist between socially valued forms of agency on the one hand and levels of income on the other, so that agency can no longer be undermined by low levels of income" (2013, 141). Failure to pay heed to agency poverty and to establish "targets" for empowerment will potentially further alienate those in poverty and reify the social and political divisions between those who have income-agency and those who do not, despite the best effort at MFP of a broad class of stakeholders.

We can use Melish's structure as a base but must enhance its democratic foundation. To begin we must understand the potential government-citizen dynamics as they pertain to the mobilization and participation of the poor. We conceptualize four kinds of engagement and relationship: authentic participation, symbolic/fake participation, controlled participation, and tokenistic participation.

Figure 7.1 introduces core elements of this participatory framework using the language of empowerment and manipulation. Rather than conceive of empowerment and manipulation as opposing forces, our framework considers

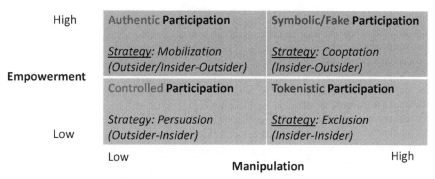

Figure 7.1. Empowerment-Manipulation Matrix

them to be linked, and with different strategies of engagement depending on the level of empowerment and level of manipulation.

Table 7.1 applies the seven dichotomies or battlefronts, as we termed them, to the four participation forms. We further assign a point value to each participation form based on the desirability of participation characteristics, such that mass competence, informed judgment, active citizens, citizenship, quality of participation, inclusivity, and empowerment each have an assigned value of 1, and expertise, transparency, volunteers, consumerism, quantity of participation, representation, and tolerance of ignorance have an assigned value of 0. A combination of quantity and quality of participation has a value of 2. We do this to suggest the MFP or participation forms are unequal with

Table 7.1. Participation Strategies Scorecard

	Mobilization	Cooptation	Persuasion	Exclusion
Expertise (E) vs. Mass Competence (MC)	MC (1)	E (0)	E (0)	E (0)
Transparency (T) vs. Informed Judgment (IJ)	IJ (1)	T (0)	IJ (1)	------ (−1)
Volunteers (V) vs. Active Citizens (AC)	AC (1)	V (0)	AC (1)	------ (−1)
Consumerism (CON) vs. Citizenship (CIT)	CIT (1)	CON (0)	CIT (1)	----- (−1)
Quantity (QT) vs. Quality (QL)	QT & QL (2)	QL (1)	QL (1)	----- (−1)
Representation (R) vs. Inclusivity (I)	I (1)	R (0)	I (1)	R (0)
Tolerance of Ignorance (TI) vs. Empowerment (EM)	EM (1)	TI (0)	EM (1)	TI (0)
	8	1	6	−4

respect to potential for reducing agency and status poverty, and moving the poor out of included-out status.

Mobilization

This is an optimal MFP strategy that has high empowerment and low manipulation. It is a strategy of outsiders engaging outsiders, or the poor and related stakeholders engaging each other. Government is not a part of this relationship. The action is one of mobilization and possible revolution. This may include professional stakeholders and interest groups influencing the poor, but success of the approach rests on the vibrancy of the mass. Importantly, this is a position in which government and citizen are not working together; it is an adversarial position but it is a position that potentially builds trusting relationships across individuals and other professional stakeholders. This is fundamentally Melish's MFP design of broad stakeholder participation, however without some level of "coordination" by a federal office.

This strategy specifically seeks to build relations across poor and non-poor citizens, to reduce status poverty and agency poverty in the quest for solutions to subsistence poverty. It prioritizes mass competence over expertise, informed judgment over potentially overwhelming transparency, active citizens who can engage the state over volunteers who can assist the state, citizenship over consumerism, inclusivity over representation, and empowerment over tolerance of ignorance. With respect to prioritizing quantity or quality of participation, this strategy pursues both equally, seeking as wide array of citizens, poor and non-poor, to participate while building their capacity to enable a meaningful participatory experience.

Cooptation

Another strategy is one of insiders engaging outsiders. Government officials proactively develop participatory processes through which citizens, including the poor, are brought into decision-making, policymaking, and program implementation. The action here is one of cooptation, as citizens are integrated into existing power and authority structures. This is an action of government and citizen working together. The risk with this approach is what some democracy observers have called "fake democracy" (Snyder 2011). This is the appearance of inclusion and involvement without any actual power granted to citizens. It is a form of placation and not of empowerment, or at least it has the potential to be (Arnstein 1969).

This strategy seeks, on the part of government or another elite group seeking influence over non-elite and poor, while giving the impression of power. It stands opposite the strategy of mobilization across elements, as an elite controls the process with only symbolic granting of power to the poor. It is a strategy that prioritizes expertise over mass competence, potentially overwhelming transparency over informed judgment, volunteers over active citizens, consumerism over citizenship, flawed representation over inclusivity, and tolerance of ignorance over empowerment. The one area that is potentially strong in this strategy is a focus on quality of participation over quantity. Not many poor might be selected to serve on advisory boards, but those who are selected will be provided tools to be successful in this role as representatives of a much larger demographic.

Persuasion

Another strategy is that of outsiders engaging insiders. These are citizens, including the poor, working to push inside governmental processes, to potentially change those processes, and to generate better policies. This is an action of persuasion. This is perhaps what was intended in the pure form of MFP—it may start with insiders engaging outward but ultimately leads to outsiders empowered to reach in, to ask hard questions about poverty, and to make meaningful contributions to poverty eradication efforts. In sum, the poor achieve more equal standings of agency with their fellow citizens. It is a strategy where expertise is prioritized over mass competence, in that the gateway is controlled by an elite/expert class, but much of the rest aligns with the mobilization strategy: informed judgment is prioritized over potentially overwhelming transparency, active citizens over volunteers, citizenship over consumerism, quality of participation over quantity of participation, inclusivity over representation, and empowerment over tolerance of ignorance.

Exclusion

Last is the strategy of insiders engaging insiders. These are government officials engaging each other and/or professional stakeholders and interest groups but not the people directly. The action here is one of exclusion and, like the action of mobilization, it does not involve government and citizen working together. This is perhaps most like what the Community Action Programs and MFP looked like in 1963. The people, the poor, were used as pawns but the hard work of policy negotiation was relegated to professional stakeholder groups, pressure groups, and interest groups. It is perhaps what the policymaking environment looks most like in 2017 as well with negotiations of healthcare reform and other poverty measures.

Ultimately, what is required is a dynamic middle, integrating across all four of these actions: mobilization, cooptation, persuasion, and with limited exclusion. It must begin, though, with government proactively engaging institutional partners that are closest to the people: churches, universities, and the media, for example. The lack of trust in government directly means the government acting alone will not be successful. In the 21st century, MFP, and strengthened government-citizen relationships must in practice be relationships in a circle, with multiple nodes forming a strong bond.

Now, we will examine some policy ideas that can address subsistence, agency, and status poverties concurrently. In other words, we ask what are the kinds of programs that can move a person towards being fully included-in—ethically and politically, culturally and religiously, and legally.

War on Poverty and Impoverished Citizenship Policies

As discussed in chapters 5 and 6, for more than fifty years, a range of programs have been implemented to combat poverty, by providing protection to those most in need and by helping to promote those same individuals towards a potential of greater success in life. Some programs have the potential to empower those who are being served, and some have such empowerment as part of their mission, at least implicitly. The history of anti-poverty programs, however, is not largely a history of programs that explicitly target subsistence, status, and agency poverty simultaneously; the history is not a suite of programs that have actually empowered.

In this section, we suggest a set of policies that might pass this test, that allow for not a maximum *feasible* participation but a maximum *empowerment* participation. This MEP integrates across mobilization, persuasion, cooptation, with limited exclusion approaches to participation of the poor with the non-poor, bridging government, nonprofit, faith-based, and private sectors. With theses standards, we accept the foundation identified by Melish in her proposal for a 21st century MFP and build on it. To ensure fidelity to these goals, we suggest not only subsistence poverty targets specified by a national orchestrating body but agency and status poverty targets as well.

We organize our discussion of potential policy interventions according to the categories of citizenship: ethical and political, cultural and religious, and legal. Proposed policies and programs will help the poor become included-in while meeting current subsistence and future growth needs and interests. Increasing inclusion-in, we suggest, will help reduce status and agency poverty. The ideas that follow are based partially on reformulation of existing programs, and some are wholly unique. We are not writing here to promote or advocate for these solution but to suggest these are the kinds of "new thinking" that are required to truly have a war on poverty and impoverished citizenship for the 21st century.

Ethical and Political Citizenship

Volunteers in Service to America (VISTA) was an early program and remains a tool in the federal-state-local tool chest for fighting poverty. It was designed to essentially facilitate young people who were educated or in the process of receiving higher education to take their privilege and test it within communities and environments just as foreign to them as a Peace Corps volunteer would find in a developing nation. As a tool for empowering the poor and facilitating movement towards being ethically and politically included-in, VISTA can be expanded to specifically recruit volunteers who come from impoverished backgrounds.

This specific recruitment potentially accomplishes several things: (1) VISTA volunteers who serve to build the capacity of organizations that serve the poor have experienced poverty and thus can potentially better inform organizations about how to create policies and programs that are most responsive. (2) VISTA volunteers working within professional environments gain credibility and legitimacy and thus have a potential to increase their personal status along with those whom they symbolically, at least, represent. (3) VISTA volunteers receive an education award at the end of their year of service that they can use to pay off student loan debt or pay tuition for future education, thus helping them individually to find opportunity through education to grow into the economy. (4) VISTA volunteers are exposed to the power of the volunteer to make a difference in communities, thus decreasing agency poverty, and through social networks, potentially increasing agency of others. (5) VISTA volunteers work within diverse communities, and the VISTA community itself is socio-economically diverse, thus facilitating changed perceptions of non-poor volunteers of those who come from impoverished backgrounds and vice versa, overall shifting agency and status poverties in a mutual quest to mitigate the harms and prevent where possible subsistence poverty.

We can also look at variations of VISTA that link not to government and nonprofit organizations but to other civic advocacy groups, including interest groups and political party organizations. The political and policymaking processes in the United States thrive on the work of the grassroots, as advocates or lobbyists or information intermediaries. With the aim not to heal poverty as the only societal goal, a version of VISTA can be established that specifically places poor and non-poor volunteers in political organizations. We can call this a C-VISTA: Campaign VISTA. They are still serving America but not in the nonprofit context; they are serving America by helping within the policymaking community. C-VISTA volunteers learn the sills of advocacy, in Democrat and Republican organizations, liberal and conservative, and all other partisan and ideological variations. The benefits can be achieved as stated with respect to VISTA, with the addition of developed agency and status within the policymaking community.

Another intervention we can devise borrows from the idea of a philan-thropic giving circle (Eikenberry 2009). Giving circles consist of a group of people of various sizes who pool financial donations and, through some democratic or consensus process, determine where to invest them in their community or elsewhere. They leverage the power of multiple contributors to potentially rival the power of a single wealthy contributor. Some giving circles have developed some exclusionary practices, despite their democratic intentions, but the pure model is participatory and potentially empowering.

Giving circles of the poor can be created with low-entry fee; for example, a circle can be created whereby individuals agree to give $10 per month. If 200 people sign up, $2,000 per month or $24,000 per year can be generated for group decision about where to invest. For $24,000 per year, citizens can fund or help fund a healthy cooking class in their neighborhood, repair park or playground equipment in their neighborhood, improve neighborhood lighting, or anything of the kind. The process can be facilitated by a local community foundation to ensure appropriate use and management of funds, with potential for federal or state government matching funds to encourage individual participation.

This process can build agency and status for the poor, give them a direct role in raising money for their own initiatives and determining how those funds are spent. They can, through this process, align their funds with exist-ing programs or initiatives of government or nonprofit organizations, which demonstrates the power of leveraging scarce resources to have a multiplying effect on community impact. Finally, their investment can have a material benefit in mitigating the effects of subsistence poverty within their com-munity.

A variation of this model can permit non-poor to also contribute, so long as the convener community foundation or other entity monitors and ensures compliance with democratic process rules. Namely, all voices must have equal weight and all donors must have equal vote, regardless of economic status or value of the contribution. Again, federal or state funds can be used as a match to incentivize individual and whole community participation.

Of course, $10 per month might itself be unreachable or not feasible for those who require every cent every week. As such, a "giving time circle" can be established with the same basic parameters. Rather than commit $10 per month to invest financially in a project or initiative, an individual can commit to give ten hours per month. As donors of time, the circle decides through democratic or consensus process how to invest their volunteer hours in the community. For instance, the donors can give their assembled time to a food bank, homeless shelter, community garden, school, park, or to some other special initiative that strikes the donors as most significant for their neighborhood or community. To engage the federal government in such an effort would be beneficial and possible through VISTA, engaging a volunteer to establish the framework and implement the regular community volunteer initiatives.

Cultural and Religious Citizenship

To become culturally included-in requires acceptance of "non-normal" behaviors, values, and beliefs to be accepted by the "mainstream." As such programs and initiatives should be structured in a way to allow the poor to develop skills for entering "mainstream" society while also giving opportunity for the non-poor to experience poverty. There are existing programs that can be restructured to support these goals and new initiatives that can be developed.

For example, we can look at the minimum wage debate. On the surface, this is not a debate about cultural norms, but culture is sustained and perpetuated when wage levels are low and subsistence becomes an ongoing challenge. Proponents of raising the minimum wage to $15 per hour or something like it seek to make sure nobody who works should live in poverty. As previously discussed, this is a complicated debate made more complicated with some philosophical argument: why pay a decent wage for a low-skill/no-skill worker? In cases where that no-skill/low-skill position is occupied by a teenager looking for some first-time spending cash, the question becomes very practical.

How then can we reconceive of the minimum wage debate to satisfy the desire to provide not only something better approximating a living wage but to provide opportunity for upward mobility? In personal responsibility parlance, how do we help those who want to help themselves, without necessarily affixing high costs to help those who either do not need help (e.g., the teenager) or who have no interest in advancement?

One approach is to build on existing policy infrastructure; maintain the minimum wage at a level appropriate to the skill level of the job, but provide government tax incentives for businesses that conduct on-the-job training for those who are most in need, with the aim that the training will lead to promotions within the organization or even promotions to a different organization, at higher pay commensurate with experience and skill. These are not new ideas, but they may represent more specific targeting of tax incentive funding to provide training and promotion opportunities for upward mobility.

The link of this to cultural inclusion is two-fold. First, helping systematically and regularly put poor individuals through professional development with the intent of rising them through the ranks, introduces more people within an organizational hierarchy to unique norms and values that are associated with having limited means. Second, those who proceed through such training to advance will be exposed to professional norms and values that challenge their own experiences, thus allowing individuals to grow, escaping all forms of poverty as they do.

Minimum wage is essentially a subsidy program; it is difficult to ask small businesses in particular to hit these targets, when money might better be invested in training personnel for advancement. Perhaps then we consider a two-tier system: for businesses that invest in training their people, they will have a lower minimum wage standard; those who do not, they will have a higher standard. In either case, businesses will support their people: one through maintenance, one through growth. Businesses exercise their obligation but in a way that makes sense for their business growth.

The poor do not necessarily need to rely on the business ventures of others to earn their livelihood, have others learn about them, and to allow them to learn about others. In a similar way as we can develop initiatives to encourage the poor and non-poor to bind together in philanthropic giving circles, we can consider programs that allow impoverished individuals or groups to become social entrepreneurs. Social entrepreneurship is the act of doing well for oneself while doing good for others. The policy and legal terrain remains ambiguous around the status and characteristics of social entrepreneurial ventures, and so there is opportunity to craft new tax or other incentive structures. Such structures could facilitate, for example, poor and non-poor individuals to bind together and create a new venture that returns proceeds to specific neighborhoods or community initiatives that help poor individuals develop and impoverished communities transform.

We see cultural inclusion strategies in workplaces and through business ventures. In a similar way, there are cultural inclusion strategies that can be developed within other institutional settings, including housing and schools. For example, in housing, we learned in chapter 5, there are initiatives to create mixed-income neighborhoods through HOPE VI grants and other funding programs. We can build on this concept and create neighborhoods or housing units that are not only mixed-income but with a civic purpose, thus addressing subsistence needs through housing support, status needs through blending across socio-economic strata, and agency needs by embedding a civic purpose as part of the identity of the neighborhood, block, condo or apartment building, or other segment of the community.

This is perhaps akin to Living Learning Centers (LLC) that are found within university residence halls (Bryer 2014; Edwards and McKelfresh 2002; Inkelas and Weisman 2003; Stassen 2003). These are designated floors within larger residential buildings for students that have a requirement for living on that floor, namely participation in some themed activity. For instance there can be an LLC devoted to volunteerism, environmental stewardship, animal welfare, or hunger and homelessness. Within a university environment, these themed living arrangements provide social and educational opportunities that also further enable the development of agency.

These are only a few possibilities that build on existing policy and program infrastructure and design elements to simultaneously address subsistence, status, and agency poverty, and move the poor towards being culturally included-in within their communities. Now we turn to the least flexible form of citizenship: legal.

Legal Citizenship

To be legally excluded from full participation in society is perhaps the most difficult barrier to overcome psychologically and behaviorally. Felon enfranchisement, no drug testing for welfare recipients, work requirements that do not consider volunteering as equal to paid employment—these are some of the things can help the excluded become more included. Research tells us that those who are most likely to participate in community life are those who maintain a part of their identity with the community. To exclude the poor through laws that effectively ask them to wear the equivalent of Nathaniel Hawthorne's scarlet letter does not engender a feeling of goodwill or that of belonging and shared identity. All we can suggest here is a desire if not a need to examine these legal requirements and/or restrictions that prevent full or even partial inclusion of citizens, or that promote biased views against citizens who are poor. When societies set groups of citizens apart through such legal practices, citizens take the cues and attach their own negative perceptions that create and reinforce established stereotypes. This enables the vicious cycle of subsistence, status, and agency poverties, mutually reinforcing each other.

The same vicious cycle applies to another sub-population that, we suggest, is treated in the same manner as the poor; or, the poor are treated in the same manner as this sub-population: migrants and refugees. In the next chapter, we explore this group, applying some of the same concepts, and consider a different variation of MFP, namely that of organizing the power structure.

CHAPTER EIGHT

~

Organizing the Power Structure to Address Poverty and Refugees

In past decades, the Western World has been experiencing challenges associated with the global refugee crisis. Fragmentation of the population has occurred in nations and communities. Citizens have become more open in expressing their anti-immigrant sentiments, giving rise to xenophobia and right-wing political parties, eventually bringing social isolation and urban segregation to newcomers. Being included-out, immigrants find it difficult to be integrated into the private labor market, attain education and exercise their legal and civic rights. If the main reason to flee is war and economic well-being, in future decades more people might leave their homes to find shelter and safe place from climate change and environmental disasters. High inflow of immigrants creates new challenges to national policies of countries that aim to successfully integrate newcomers into host communities and provide safety to their population.

The link between being included-out as a poor born-and-raised citizen of a country, and being an immigrant or refugee is clear. The temptations, biases, and laws that push both groups out of mainstream society towards included-out status are grounded in perceptions, stereotypes, and fear (Chomsky 2007). Like the woman we met from the PBS series *Frontline* in the second chapter, fear of the "other" creates societal divisions, however inaccurate the perceptions that breed the fear are.

Miller (2016, 4) describes the situation for immigrants:

Controlling immigration only became an issue when the numbers arriving became large, or when the newcomers were regarded as undesirable on economic, moral, or racial grounds (or combinations of these). Thus in the Untied States, the first significant restriction imposed at [the] federal level was on Chinese immigrants in 1882, in response to concerns that Chinese men were competing with native workers for jobs, and Chinese women were working as prostitutes. In the United Kingdom, the Aliens Act of 1906 was aimed primarily at Jewish emigrants from Eastern Europe, though Chinese seamen were also targeted. In both cases supporters of immigration control used a rhetoric that denounced the low morals of the allegedly inferior races. Immigrants were acceptable, in other words . . . so long as they were of a type that posed no threat either to the morals or to the economic interests of existing citizens. And they were expected to fend for themselves. The state took no responsibility for the welfare of immigrants, who typically struggled for survival in the lowest depths of the society.

Advance the clock to today, and we witness stereotypes about immigrants and refugees born of fear and misunderstanding. We need not look beyond TED talks to see how these stereotypes play out. For instance, Yassmin Abdel-Magied (2015) asked in her talk "What does my headscarf mean to you?" She came to the stage dressed in conservative dress typically associated with Muslim women; during the talk she changed her appearance showing her uniform working on an oil rig, more casual clothes, and so on—all while wearing the headscarf. Her point: false impressions based on limited exposure to the "other" are misleading and assume more difference between people than actually exists.

At the same time, images that emerge of refugees lead to sympathy and empathic concern for the well-being of fellow human beings, such as the infamous photo of a young child's body washed up on a beach shore. Anders Fjellberg (2014) tells a story that reflects this kind of empathy. He tells the tale of two bodies that washed up on the shore, both wearing identical wetsuits. These are individuals who tried to swim to a better life as refugees across dangerous waters. The conclusion: everyone has a story and a life.

These episodes give rise to donors who will support refugee-serving organizations and may also spur the emergence of advocates for refugee causes. As with the poor, refugees and migrants are not socially, civically, or culturally embedded in society (Miller 2016). They are without agency or status, and their capacity to hold representatives to account is limited. As such, solutions to integrate and empower and reduce poverty in all its forms for refugees and migrants are the same in theme if not design as solutions to do the same for the poor.

In this chapter, we take a different example of Maximum Feasible Participation (MFP), however, to focus not on empowerment and representation but on responsiveness. This is Moynihan's interpretation of MFP as *organizing the power structure* or linking agencies across government, nonprofit, faith, and private/for-profit sectors. It is an approach that contrasts with *assisting the power structure* and *confronting the power structure*, which was more the aim of discussion in the previous chapter. In describing the scenario, we focus on refugee welcoming and integration as a specific sub-population of those experiencing subsistence, agency, and status poverty. We also apply the logic with a brief example from homeless service delivery. To review the differences in these conceptions, revisit the third chapter and table 3.1.

Organizing the Power Structure to Fight Poverty

There are two components of organizing the power structure that are relevant for poverty and related refugee integration policies: decentralization and cross-sector collaboration. We discuss each from a conceptual frame first and then apply them to the issues at hand.

Decentralization

New Public Management (NPM) emerged in the 1980s and 1990s, bringing significant changes in theoretical and practical bases of public administration. According to Hood (1991), NPM tended to slow down or reverse government growth, having shifted toward privatization and quasi-privatization, and development of automation in the production of public goods and services. Osborne and Gaebler (1993) argue that this theoretical model focused on carrying out structural decentralization and cooperating decentralized structures through market-oriented efforts.

New Public Governance (NPG) shifts the attention further from internal operations within agencies to the tools and instruments of public action through which public programs are realized (Salamon 2002). NPG extends NPM, focusing on processes of program and policy implementation that involve not only one actor—the government—but provide collaboration of multiple actors from public and private sectors. Due to the complexity of local conditions, the central government has become "hollowed out" as power has been decentralized to state and local administration (Milward and Provan 2000). Bannink and Ossewaarde (2012) describe that process as "shift in governance" or "decentralization operations responding to capacities in a material sense being shared between the central and decentralized levels of a governance constellation" (599).

Bannink and Ossewaarde (2012) identify three modes of decentralization that define the relationship between central government and decentralized levels of administration. The first two are applied to *incomplete decentralization*. First, the transfer of policy content is a mode when government shifts policymaking autonomy and implementation discretion to geographically and functionally decentralized levels of administration. The second mode is the transfer of policy resources, which is the distribution of financial and other resource risks and successes to decentralized levels of administration. The third approach is *full decentralization* when both substantial and resource competencies are transferred. Thus decentralized actors are responsible for both policy formulation and implementation and financial risks associated with the policy failure or success (Bannink and Ossewaarde 2012).

However, public managers and policymakers encounter challenges associated with decentralization. They must ensure accountability and good practices "across diverse service units in dispersed locations" and guarantee that all members of the public receive goods and services in a fair manner (Lynn, Heinrich, and Hill 2000, 243). Lynn et al. (2000) maintain that the variation in performance among decentralized units depends on the "characteristics or needs of the people served; the skills or motivations of the direct service workers; the quality of local site management; the clarity of policy direction; factors in the local environment; the extent of system-wide coordination; the strength and enforcement of performance incentives; and other structural characteristics of the system" (2000, 243). These tendencies and tools of governance to support them were not readily available or tested, as such, in the launch of the War on Poverty (Melish 2010).

We see these decentralization approaches in poverty plans dating back to the War on Poverty programs, which sought to localize development of initiatives and interventions, sometimes to the exclusion of official, democratically elected local authorities (Gillezeau 2010; Cazenave 2007). Since then, various block grant programs are specifically designed to push power at least to the state level in the United States for allocation of available resources to fight poverty, though with some strings attached. One such string is a limitation on giving social service support to immigrants who are legally in the country for fewer than five years. With this context, immigration policy itself sometimes leads to disagreements across federal, state, and local governments.

With respect to immigration policy, federal and subnational governments pursue distinct interests and values that bring a potential conflict between administrations vertically and horizontally. The federal government's interest lies in free-flowing labor market and matching immigrants at subnational levels, according to their socio-economic needs (Boushey and Luedtke 2006). The subnational governments play a key role in integration and resettlement services. Shields et al. (2016) believe that decentralization of immigration services creates disparities among immigrants depending on their location. This can be explained due to the lack of coordination between state policy-makers, who might treat newcomers differently (Giordani and Ruta 2011).

There are two principles that can guide decentralized migration policies (Hepburn and Zapata-Barrero 2014): the principle of cooperation and the principle of coherence, allocated across both vertical and horizontal multilevel relations between administrative units. Cooperation refers to the issues of common interest such as healthcare, and employment, and the need for alignment in interests. This principle, once enacted, can ensure there are no negative effects of one unit's decisions on others across the vertical and horizontal relations. The principle of coherence assumes that when actors have different interests on matters, such as education, they can work collaboratively without contradicting each other (Hepburn and Zapata-Barrero 2014).

Cross-Sector Collaboration

There is a long-standing built-in capacity for cross-sector collaboration in the United States. Alexis d'Toqueville (1840) wrote about the grassroots vibrancy of 19th century American life, consisting of like minded and interested citizens at the local level able and willing to organize themselves to enhance community life. This grassroots vibrancy has been and continues to be the backbone of nonprofit organization and voluntary association emergence in neighborhoods and communities around the country. The emergence of governance reforms, such as New Public Management that have pushed for the professionalization of nonprofit and community-based organizations, have perhaps siphoned some of the inherent grassroots energy embodied by new and emergent nonprofit organizations (Skocpol 2003; Crenson and Ginsberg 2002). Yet, the fundamental energy remains, and when combined with the professionalism, allows for the emergence of the extra-state federalism (multi-flavored wedding cake) about which we spoke in the first chapter.

Collaboration of this kind "generally involves a higher degree of mutual planning and management among peers; the conscious alignment of goals, strategies, agendas, resources, and activities; an equitable commitment of investment and capacities; and sharing risks, liabilities, and benefits. . . . Collaboration, therefore, suggests something less than authoritative coordination and something more than tacit cooperation" (Fosler 2002, as cited in Gazley 2008, 142).

With creative loosening of restrictions on government funding of faith-based organizations most particularly beginning during the George W. Bush administration, the cross-sector governance landscape today consists of both secular and faith-based organizations (Bretherton 2015; Bryer 2014b; Jackson-Elmoore, Hula, and Reese 2011; Stout 2010). The difference between secular and faith-based is minimal in terms of social service delivery sectors but vary with respect to clientele served, source of revenue, and abidance to government regulation, among other factors (Jackson-Elmoore, Hula, and Reese 2011). Whereas secular NGOs address the needs common to society, faith-based organizations tend to be more ethnic-specific, focusing on the needs of specific cultural and religious groups (Bielefeld and Cleveland 2013).

This is the context for governance systems that consist of "self-organizing networks of institutions, organizations, and actors drawn from the public, private and civil society sectors" (Musso, Weare, Oztas, and Loges 2006, 81). Collaborative governance brings new accountability and legitimacy challenges for public managers (Salamon 2002). As Melish (2010) observes, new accountability also brings new opportunity to address poverty and other social inequities, such as those associated with migrants and refugees. Public managers require skills that help them to manage nonhierarchical structures, including the complex and interdependent nature of contemporary third-party government, accompanied with the "loss of control, threats to authority, or greater difficulty in holding private organizations accountable to public standards" (Gazley and Brudney 2007, 390).

These skills allow public managers to take advantage of and effectively partner and engage with the diversity of the nonprofit sector, including the faith-sector. The sector is not only diverse with respect to secular/non-secular, community-based or federal in structure, and size; it is diverse in terms of individual organizational function. The nonprofit-government relationship can be complementary, supplementary, or adversarial (Young 1999).

Nonprofits can serve as supplements to government, when they provide public goods left unsatisfied by government. The complementary mode defines collaborative relationships between nonprofit organizations and government. An adversarial relationship is explained by advocacy behavior of nonprofits, and government pressure in controlling nonprofit organizations (Young 1999). These functions can be broken down even further to include: autonomous service providers, coordinated service allies, subsidized service provision, contractor/agent, strategic competitors, partnership, and advocate/lobbyist (Feiock and Andrew 2006). Across these functions, we also see relationships that are structured differently, according to the blending of interests across organizations (Herranz 2007), including where one sector dominates, where there is shared dominance without direct interaction, and where there is collaboration (Gidron, Kramer, and Salamon 1992).

We see examples of these functions and relation structures within the refugee and migrant response systems, and, ultimately, the nonprofit functions, appearing contradictory, are themselves complementary. Faith-organizations, for instance, can serve a supplemental role by providing food and social network support to refugees and migrants through their individual ministries; professionalized nonprofit organizations can act as collaborators through contracts to provide specific services to refugees, such as job or language training; advocacy organizations, such as Human Rights Watch, can keep a watchful eye on the whole delivery system to ensure fair and humane treatment. The same setup fits within the broader anti-poverty delivery systems; it is an organization of the power structure that leverages the unique passions, interests, and resources of the full variety of organizations active in the policy space.

Organizing the Power Structure for Refugee Integration

The immigration system in the United States has been characterized as a "melting pot" and as "swim or sink" by many observers and politicians. Immigrants have a responsibility for their own integration in the host society (Shields et al. 2016). The federal government almost solely exercises authority over both immigration control and immigrant integration policies. It is in charge of "market- and nation preserving elements of American immigration policy" (Boushey and Luedtke 2006, 217).

The U.S. Congress establishes the criteria for selecting the number and type of immigrants the country is willing to accept. Although state governments share some costs in providing settlement services in education, healthcare, and job training, they do not have the power to decide the flow of immigrants or placement of immigrants in their states.

Federal agencies partner directly with the United Nations in order to identify the number and type of refugees and immigrants, and they set an annual refugee cap. For instance, in the current year, the federal government expects only 2,000 Syrian refugees from approximately 23,000 referrals by the United Nations. The partner agencies include Department of State Bureau of Population, Refugees, and Migration (PRM) Refugee Admissions program, the Office of Refugee Resettlement (ORR) in the Department of Health and Human Services, and the Refugee Affairs Division of the United States Citizenship and Immigration Services in the Department of Homeland Security (UNHCR 2017). The federal government makes decisions upon resettlement based on three criteria: state resources, kin, whether the state already has immigrants of a particular nationality and, whether the state has voluntary agencies that manage immigrant integration.

Nonprofit-Government Relations in Settlement Services

With a high inflow of immigrants after World War II, the government of the United States sought the help of nonprofit organizations and humanitarian agencies, which have played the main role in refugee resettlement. The Refugee Act of 1980 officially established the partnerships between the federal government and resettlement agencies and also identified the role of private sector organizations (Brown and Scribner 2014). The Act also created the refugee resettlement program and a series of assistance programs through partnerships with private entities and nonprofit organizations to help refugees in transition in the United States. However, according to Brown and Scribner (2014, 101), "coordination and information sharing between these agencies and with resettlement agencies has been less than optimal." Receiving communities and resettlement agencies were burdened with the lack of support and resources to assist refugees (ibid.).

Currently, the migrant settlement services are mostly provided by community and faith-based organizations, supported by government grants (Sheilds et al. 2016). There are three types of nongovernmental organizations that deal with immigrant resettlement in the United States: Voluntary Agencies (VOLAGs), mutual assistance associations (MAAs), and support agencies (Nawyn 2006). The State Department establishes cooperative contracting agreements with VOLAGs. Although state government is not involved in making a decision regarding resettlement and integration, the primary funding for VOLAGS comes from both federal and state levels of government.

VOLAGS consist of nine private and one state agency: Church World Service (CWS), Ethiopian Community Development Council (ECDC), Episcopal Migration Ministries (EMM), Hebrew Immigrant Aid Society (HIAS), International Rescue Committee (IRC), U.S. Committee for Refugees and Immigrants (USCRI), Lutheran Immigration and Refugee Services (LIRS), United States Conference of Catholic Bishops (USCCB), and World Relief Corporation (WR) (Office of Refugee Resettlement 2017). The majority of organizations are faith-based, nonsectarian or ethnically-related (Wright 1981). According to Nawyn (2006, 1512), VOLAGs "contract directly with State Department to resettle a set number of refugees, and the national offices, in turn, assign those refugees to their local offices in various cities." There are 350 federal subcontractors each affiliated with

VOLAGs in 190 cities in the United States. According to USAspending. gov, government grants account for more than 90 percent of the total revenue for ECDC, LIRS, and USCRI. Although some VOLAGs advocate for changes in immigration law in Congress and bureaucracy, receiving most of their funds from governmental grants dictating them to remain as government agents and service providers.

The second group of nonprofits is MAAs. Although these nonprofits differ from VOLAGs, they are affiliated to at least one of the voluntary agencies. MAAs are secular ethnic organizations that serve particular immigrant groups. These organizations are less faith oriented, and they provide a broader range of services that help with refugee integration into society (Nawyn 2006).

The third group is support agencies. Support agencies do not provide resettlement services, however, they provide any type of assistance to refugees. They include faith-based organizations, secular nonprofits and government agencies that provide cultural integration, recruit volunteers who collect items to furnish refugees' apartments, provide transportation to job interviews and other appointments. The support agencies act as autonomous service providers, advocacy groups, and collaborative partners with local and state governments. When it comes to collaborative partnerships, the City of Philadelphia shows the evidence of shared responsibility between the public and non-governmental sectors in the delivery of language access services. Through collaborative partnerships, municipal government and local nonprofit organizations ensure that immigrants receive services despite their language abilities (Wilson 2013). Mexican immigrant non-profit organizations located across the United States facilitate the integration of Mexican immigrants and, at the same time, preserve their cultural heritage. Mexican civil society organizations receive most of their funds from the Mexican government, which oblige them to follow Mexican government interests and the U.S. rules.

In this case, the distribution of power is federal government dominant in enacting immigration laws and providing funds for services. Indeed, states share some financial and other risks for the immigrant integration by providing funds to local nongovernmental organizations. The majority of observed relationships between government and nonprofits can be described as Subsidized Service Provisions or Contractor/Agent interaction. Shields et al. (2016, 21) argue that "prioritization of tasks required by the government do not always match newcomers' needs and compels nonprofits to disregard other important roles including advocacy and research." Richmond and Shields (2005) suggest that the integration services are in a high need of policy attention. The government-funded activities are short-term. Networks and collaborative partnerships across sectors, based on a blend of functions and relations, are needed in order to provide long-term services for newcomers and host societies.

Organizing the Power Structure for Homelessness

We can apply the same theory and logic organizing the power structure to another poverty-related policy issue: homelessness. To demonstrate this point, we share data from research conducted on a homeless services network in a county located near our university. Nonprofit, government, and faith-based organizations responded to a survey that enabled us to map referral relationships across agencies that have some role in meeting the complex needs of homeless individuals and families. Respondents were given a scenario or portrait of a family in poverty, homeless, with multiple needs, such as job training, medical care, education services for children, housing, drug rehabilitation, and so on. We then asked respondents to first indicate which of the needed services their agency can provide, and then we asked to whom they referred the family in the event they could not meet all of the needs.

Unlike refugee services, there is no overarching federal framework that necessarily constrains local responses. There are federal sources of funding for housing, drug treatment, job training, education, and so on, and these laws certainly can influence how local advocates, nonprofit organizations, and governments seek to work together. On the whole, solutions to homelessness and caring for those who are homeless are a local obligation. The ability to organize the power structure is vital for successful response in providing the "basic" protection programs previously described, let alone seeking to promote homeless individuals to a place of self-sufficiency.

Figure 8.1 shows the referral network for homeless service delivery in this community. We can see here a significant organization of the power structure problem: the network is not at all cohesive, and there is no clear pattern of relationship across agencies. Lacking sense from this perspective, we can imagine the frustration and disempowerment that occurs for the homeless family seeking access to the multiple services they may need. With such fragmentation, it is more likely a family will "drop out" before getting to all the places they should within the service delivery network.

This fragmentation is perhaps more pronounced in homeless services delivery than in refugee services, as there are more agencies—government and nonprofit—that are active in providing care to homeless as a distinct population than there are for immigrants and refugees. Though there is overlap

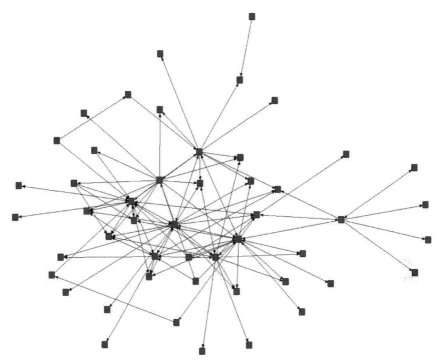

Figure 8.1. Fragmented Power Structure for Homeless Support

between these populations, in the social services arena, they are divided. Yet, the populations are similar, as discussed at the top of this chapter: both are included-out from core aspects of society. Homeless are perhaps in a worse situation, in that they are more likely to lack something that is the ticket to all manner of legal, ethical, or cultural expressions of citizenship: identification (Izaguirre 2017; Wiltz 2017).

Toward a Stronger Organization

Decentralization is an important factor that gives political, economic, and administrative authority to local governments to enact laws, build partnerships and provide services that address the needs of newcomers. However, we see in the case of immigration, refugee integration, and homelessness services that decentralized government systems do not necessarily lead to decentralized governance processes.

In the United States, where the immigration system is centralized, there are some examples how nonprofit organizations collaborate with local governments in addressing the needs of immigrant communities, for example, the case of language access services in the City of Philadelphia. Other U.S. nonprofit organizations that serve immigrant needs, such as VOLAGS, MAAs, or support agencies receive most of their funding from the federal and state government. This constrains their ability to flexibly distribute funding and advocate for the rights of immigrants.

Trust and social capital are the main prerequisites for partnerships and network building (Borgatti and Foster 2003; Provan, Veazie, 2005; Provan, Fish, Staten, and Teufel-Shone, and Sydow 2007). As Provan et al. (2005) claim, trust-based relationships, formal or informal, facilitate achievement of goals in addressing complex, wicked societal problems that cannot be accomplished through contracts, or by a single organization.

The local governments do not have enough resources and capacities to support collaborative activities of nonprofit organizations in matters of immigrant integration, and in the case of homeless service delivery, there are trust barriers as well as constraints imposed through competition for scarce resources. Thus, the relationships remain contract based, with nonprofits relying on state and federal government grants and often standing against each other than in coordination, cooperation, or collaboration with each other. Contracting creates a principal-agent problem when government tries to realize its goals and objectives through nonprofits. Difficulties in monitoring nonprofit performance lead to more restrictive and formalized contracts between organizations, which bring more rigid regulations and interference in the autonomy of nonprofit organizations—a vicious cycle that ultimately interferes with the ability to flexibly provide service to those in need.

Figure 8.2 depicts an alternative to the fragmentation, an organization of the power structure that has the real possibility of providing seamless services to those in need. In this network depiction, homeless individuals or refugees and immigrants, as the case may be, have multiple access points to the service delivery network, with each access point only one step away from a network hub. Getting lost in the system is not an option. This is an alternative MFP, not of the people, per se, but of the agencies seeking to serve the people. Combined with the Maximum Empowerment Participation discussed in the previous chapter, the opportunity to wage a war on poverty and impoverished citizenship for citizens, non-citizens, refugees, and others becomes possible and, to counter Ronald Reagan, a war in which poverty would not win.

In the next chapter, we bring the wars abroad and ask how well the frameworks developed in this and the previous chapter could fit in other countries, including the Netherlands, Finland, Lithuania, Canada, and Mexico.

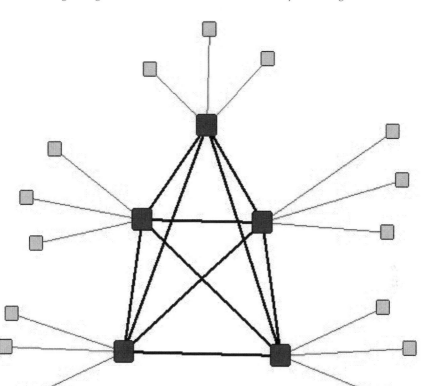

Figure 8.2. Improving the Organization of the Power Structure

We select these as "concept test" countries given their diverse geographies, histories, and political and governance structures. It is our contention that the framework developed around Maximum Empowerment Participation and MFP as organizing the power structure are more universal than context-specific, though the path towards implementation of ideas and ideals will vary greatly given diverse socio-political traditions and historical legacies.

CHAPTER NINE

~

The Wars on Poverty and Impoverished Citizenship at Home and Abroad

A report by Oxfam, published in January 2017, has a big headline that should challenge the rational and emotional thinking of every man, woman, and child around the world: "An Economy for the 99%." It is a report on income inequality and suggests in no uncertain terms that inequality and poverty is a problem around the world, and nothing short of an overhaul of our economic models and government policies will create a more globally stable and fair environment for the masses. In the report, they quote former U.S. president, Barack Obama: "A world where 1% of humanity controls as much wealth as the bottom 99% will never be stable" (Oxfam 2017, 2).

The report authors cite a number of statistics to build their argument, including (ibid.):

- Since 2015, the richest 1% has owned more wealth than the rest of the planet.
- Eight men now own the same amount of wealth as the poorest half of the world.
- Over the next 20 years, 500 people will give over $2.1 trillion to their heirs—a sum larger than the GDP of India, a country of 1.3 billion people.
- The incomes of the poorest 10% of people increased by less than $3 a year between 1988 and 2011, while the incomes of the richest 1% 182 as much.

- In the United States, new research by economist Thomas Piketty shows that over the last 30 years the growth in the incomes of the bottom 50% has been zero, whereas incomes of the top 1% have grown 300%.
- In Vietnam, the country's richest man earns more in a day than the poorest person earns in 10 years.

Thus far within the pages of this book, we have focused mostly on poverty and policies—the war on poverty and impoverished citizenship—in the United States. With these broader data as context, we turn in this chapter to examination of efforts of other countries to combat poverty and/or to ensure those who are living in poverty can also manage to do so while living with at least a modicum of dignity.

This idea of poverty with dignity is an issue around the globe and one that binds together across cultures and material costs of living. It is the same issue that is born from high levels of agency and status poverty. In a study of rural Uganda and India, urban China, Pakistan, South Korea, and small town and urban Norway—as diverse a collection of societies as any—Walker, Kyomuhendo, Chase, and Choudhry (2013) document variations of shame self-imposed by and other-imposed on the poor. Shame, as they report, led across these cultures and places to "pretense, withdrawal, self-loathing, othering, despair, depression, thoughts of suicide and generally to reductions in personal efficacy" (215). These are the very essence of the included-out citizen. They reflect a tendency towards social isolation, feelings of exclusion, and detachment from social and/or professional networks that could help lift a person up (Bierbaum and Gassmann 2016). Shame of this kind perpetuates stereotypes (Underlid 2005) and deepens the societal divide rather than heals it through elimination of status and agency poverty (Chase and Walker 2012).

In this chapter we examine several country case examples, seeking both to suggest the ideas at the foundation of Maximum Empowerment Participation and Maximum Feasible Participation as organizing the power structure are relevant outside the United States, and to provide for necessary adaptation of these ideas to other cultural and political settings. Specifically, we examine the following cases: (1) implementation of the Participation Act in the Netherlands beginning in 2015, which establishes participation-in-society requirements for any person receiving social benefits, (2) basic income experimentation in Finland, with some broader context from other countries, (3) poverty in the post-Soviet state of Lithuania, and (4) refugee integration practices in Canada and Mexico. All are presented with a contrast to the case of the United States, which, as a comparative example, can suggest both uniqueness of the American experience and potential for more universal norms (Brady and Burroway 2012), such as the kind endorsed by Oxfam (2017). Table 9.1 present as overview of different issues and approaches as related to the Netherlands, Finland, and Lithuania.

The Netherlands: Participation Act

The TANF and SNAP programs in the United States give flexibility to state governments to determine eligibility, but federal rules establish standards

Table 9.1. Comparison of International Experiences

Country	Description of Experience	Comparison to United States
Netherlands	The Participation Act requires social welfare benefit recipients must meet expectation of participating in society through employment, job seeking, and/ or volunteering.	Volunteering as an option to fulfill work requirements does not exist within the United States, and the system in the Netherlands focuses more on the whole person, promoting both economic self-sufficiency and prevention of social exclusion.
Finland	Pilot testing a basic income scheme in which 2,000 people are receiving approximately $600 per month for two years without strings, including work requirement.	Most debate in the United States focuses not on basic income schemes but minimum wage mandates that are passed on to private employers.
Lithuania	National strategy document establishes core values for addressing social exclusion associated with poverty: "The society must recognize the rights of socially marginalized people, helping them to maintain dignity and play a full part in the society, be active participants as regards social inclusion policies and related actions; it also has to help combatting the stereotypes and stigma, to preserve and enhance the quality of life, social wellbeing, especially as regards children, and equal opportunities for all" (Lietuva 2030 2012, 9–10).	American governments have expressed similar ideals but without full success across the country, resulting in social divisions and fragmentation. Lack of success in this regard can provide lessons for countries like Lithuania.

and work requirements in order to receive benefits. Such requirements are not intended to be punitive or demeaning, though they have the high potential to be just those things; they are intended to ensure accountability and to promote recipients of service to get back into the workforce, if they are able, as quickly as possible.

In the Netherlands, the Participation Act has a similar function with some of the same ambiguities and negative externalities that are not designed but still happen. Ultimately, the Participation Act establishes a goal that every person should contribute to a participatory society, whatever their individual abilities and/or limitations. As such, supporters of the law have empowering aspirations; the part of the law on which we focus here is that addressing recipients of social welfare benefits. Benefit recipients must meet some expectations of participating in society through employment, job searching, and/or volunteering. Failure to participate in these ways could result in denial of benefits, reduction in benefits, or fines (Barnhoorn 2017).

Benefits provided through the act are generally sufficient to pay for food and housing costs but without any added flexibility in entertainment spending or to manage emergency situations (Bierbaum and Gassmann 2016). A more critical review of the act, from a protection benefits perspective (see chapter 5) is that the social safety net has deteriorated thanks to the "accumulation of inspection, monitoring and sanctions" (Barnhoorn 2017).

Yet, the requirements for working, seeking work, and volunteering appear to have some benefits. Volunteering, in particular, has a benefit that is not recognized in laws of the United States, which include "being in contact with others, contributing to a societal purpose having a meaning for and being valued by other people, being active, and structuring one's day, and keeping on learning and developing" (Bierbaum and Gassmann 2016, 3). Even with these acknowledged positive benefits, though, volunteering in a field that neither allows an individual to use existing skills nor permits the individual to develop new skills is a potential waste of time and effort.

These concerns lead to the flexibility afforded by the act for cities to design experiments with rigorous evaluation to develop innovative approaches to maintain a safety net while preparing individuals for reintegration into the workforce and mainstream society more generally. The process of approving and implementing local experiments is still in its infancy, and there will be much to write at later dates about these efforts.

Unique in the Netherlands, however, and what can be learned in the United States, is the focus on the whole person: concern for economic self-sufficiency and prevention of social exclusion. That these questions are actively asked is a contrast to the development of "war on poverty" kinds of programs in the United States. The metaphor of "war" would perhaps not at all be apt in the context of the Netherlands, as the metaphor gives the impression of carpet bombing the drivers of poverty: jobs, family structure, and teen pregnancy, for example. Though the same stereotypes of the lazy, shiftless poor, and popular depictions that implicitly or explicitly shame the poor, exist in the Netherlands as they do in the United States, the approach to address poverty is less carpet bombing than hand-holding. That is, there seems to be at least a bit more concern in Dutch society for treating agency and status poverty. That said, the application of Maximum Empowerment Participation and the cross-sector collaboration (e.g., organizing the power structure) would fit here within a context that is perhaps more favorable for such efforts than in the United States.

Basic Income in Finland

In the United States, active debate shows the idea of the minimum wage or a living wage, which are government mandates placed on private employers. The issue generates substantial debate that is both substantive and ideological; it is the kind of issue that cannot be addressed simply. In some European countries, an even more bold idea has captured the imaginations of policymakers and advocates for the poor: basic income. In Finland, the government is implementing a trial program in which 2,000 people are receiving approximately $600 every month for two years. There are no strings attached, including work requirements. If a person gets a job, they do not lose the benefit (Independent Staff 2017).

The unconditional basic income (UBI) model is universal, given to the individual, unconditional, and of sufficient amount to provide a basic standard of living. Ideally it prevents subsistence poverty and gives opportunity to individuals without ample means otherwise to participate fully in society (Basic Income Earth Network 2017). The idea has been offered in various forms, including the Finnish model, and an alternative lump sum model. For instance, on the occasion of a person's 21st birthday, she would receive $10,000 to be invested or spent in any way desired: education cost, property investment, business development, car purchase, et cetera. The difference is a model of basic income versus stakeholding (Ackerman, Alstott, and Van Parij 2006). Though the potential affect of both models on empowered citizenship, status poverty, agency poverty, and so on are academic exercises at this point without either fully implemented anywhere, there is strong logic to suggest with basic income needs met without condition, individuals will be able to engage more freely and with more equal standing in social and democratic life (Ackerman, Alstott, and Van Parij 2006).

A public opinion poll conducted from April 21 to May 5, 2017 in twelve countries (Canada, France, Germany, Italy, Spain, United Kingdom, United States, Belgium, Mexico, Poland, Serbia, and Sweden) found generally positive support for the ideas and principles that undergird basic income plans, though more so in some countries than in others. Respondents were asked if they agreed or disagreed (or neither) with each of the following statements, with key findings summarized in table 9.2 (Ipsos 2017):

Curious in these data are the relatively low levels of support for government paying a basic income to all citizens but general concurrence for the potential benefits of the basic income (alleviate poverty, more time with family). The flip side is concern for the costs of the basic income, which play into stereotypes of the poor (make people more reliant on government, discourage paid employment). Across most questions there are 20–30 percent

Table 9.2. Global Comparative Support for Basic Income Plans

Statement	Key Findings (countries listed in order of highest to lowest percentage)
The government should pay all residents in [country] a basic income in the form of free and unconditional money in addition to any income received elsewhere.	60% or above agree: Poland 50–59% agree: Germany, Mexico, Italy 40% or below agree: United States, United Kingdom, Spain, France
Basic income will help to alleviate poverty in [country].	60% or above agree: Poland, Canada 50–59% agree: Germany, United States, Belgium, Mexico, Sweden, United Kingdom, Spain
Basic income will allow people to spend more time with their families.	60% or above agree: Poland, Germany, United States, Canada 50–59% agree: Mexico, Belgium, Sweden, United Kingdom, Spain
Basic income will allow people to be more involved in their local communities.	50–59% agree: Poland, Canada 40% or below agree: Spain, France
Basic income will make people reliant on the state for income.	60% or above agree: United States, France, Mexico, Poland, Spain, Canada 50–59% agree: United Kingdom, Belgium, Sweden, Italy
Basic income will discourage people from being in or seeking paid employment.	60% or above agree: United States, France 50–59% agree: Spain, Mexico, Poland, Germany, United Kingdom, Canada, Belgium, Italy
Basic income will increase taxation to unaffordable levels.	60% or above agree: France 50–59% agree: United States, Mexico, Belgium, Canada, Spain

or more undecided, which suggests education (or manipulation) in either direction can sway popular opinion (Ipsos 2017).

It is for this reason that a pilot test of the kind happening in Finland is valuable. Though the Fins have a unique and generous social security system in place, thus making any findings here less than transferable to hypothesize the effect in any other country, the pilot can still provide insight. For instance, an early finding from the pilot is that stress levels of the poor have decreased and overall mental health might be enhanced, particularly as the funding is provided without stress of continually seeking employment (Independent Staff 2017). The system provides flexibility to the individual, which can enable those things that are deemed beneficial: more time with family, more time in community (Ipsos 2017).

Poverty in Post-Soviet States: Lithuania

The United States is unique in its poverty policies, political culture, and historical norms. As such, any comparison to derive lessons should be undertaken with caution. However, Lithuania might be particularly beneficial as a comparison nation for civics and the civics of poverty. Bryer and Medina (2017, 521) make this claim in their work:

> [W]e raise the unique comparison between a large nation with vast experience (good and bad) in democratic and republican practice and a small nation whose size does not represent the spirit of the people to create something special in this land riddled with complex and oppressive history. We offer the perhaps unorthodox claim and argument that the strong and mighty can learn more from the small and emergent rather than the reverse.

With the same logic, we offer Lithuania as a case building from the bottom up, following independence at the time of the collapse of the Soviet Union in 1990, ascension to European Union membership in 2004, and joining the single currency in 2014. During the Soviet period, Lithuania maintained one of the most industrialized economies of the union; this industrial capacity provided raw material for transition to a capitalist economy but the process of privatization without protection for individual workers led to significant poverty for specific sub-populations, such as elderly, former employees of industrial work centers, and individuals working in education, agriculture, and culture (Dvorak 2015).

At the turn of the 21st century, following a banking crisis that saw large banks holding 25 percent of deposits enter bankruptcy, the official poverty rates were approximately 27 percent in rural areas and 11 percent in urban areas. As of 2010, approximately 33 percent of Lithuanian citizens report to have experienced poverty risk or social exclusion (Dvorak 2015).

The response of the Lithuanian government is embedded within a national strategy document, Lithuania 2030. In describing the idea of a smart society that includes the country's approximately 3 million citizens, the authors write (Lietuva 2030 2012, 9–10):

> The Smart Society is a happy society, which seeks greater personal and economic security and dynamism, as well as fairer income distribution, cleaner environment, better social and political inclusion, better access to education and training, skills improvement and good public health. The society must recognize the rights of socially marginalized people, helping them to maintain dignity and play a full part in the society, be active participants as regards social inclusion policies and related actions; it also has to help combatting the stereotypes and stigma, to preserve and enhance the quality of life, social wellbeing, especially as regards children, and equal opportunities for all.

As we have seen in the cases of the Netherlands and in the United States, Lithuania seeks to empower local authorities and engage other sectors in addressing these concerns of social exclusion. Unlike the Netherlands and United States, however, local authorities and civil society organizations are not highly developed, and there remains much need for capacity building. As such, any effort to empower through decentralization requires substantial preparatory work and ongoing resource commitments to ensure sustainability (Bryer and Medina 2017).

Social exclusion, or existence of included-out citizens, is certainly a challenge in Lithuania. The introduction of refugees from non-Eastern European countries is creating additional pressures that must be confronted. Within the United States, we discuss policies and programs that put included-in and included-out citizens together, standing as one, with common purpose and in structured ways. The same can be achieved in Lithuania, with the impetus to create these dialogic moments across existing and emergent societal divisions before they reach the level of disrepair that exists within American society (Bryer and Medina 2017).

Overall, Lithuanian officials seem to be using the "right" rhetoric around volunteerism, civic engagement, smart societies, social inclusion, and so on. These are similar ideas presented within the wars on poverty and impoverished citizenship in the United States. In Lithuania, the opportunity is to build these institutions while learning from the mistakes in the United States and other longer-surviving democracies. Lithuanians must, of course, contend with the historical legacies of communism and Soviet rule, which still run currents through the society (Pop-Eleches and Tucker 2017) and which may only fade as the older generations give way in leadership to the younger generations who are trained and educated in ways unique to their parents and grandparents.

Refugee Integration in Canada and Mexico

Building on the previous chapter, we offer now comparative discussion on organizing the power structure to assist immigrants, both poor and not poor, but all generally included-out in some form. As comparison to the United States, we look at two divergent examples: Mexico, a sometimes final destination and sometimes pass through for migrants from Central America, and Canada, which maintains a refugee policy considerably more liberal compared to that espoused by the Trump administration in the United States.

The Case of Canada

Politicians and scholars recognize the Canadian immigration system as effective due to its regionalization, marketization, and decentralization. "Boosting economic competitiveness, commodifying immigrants and "selling," de-centralizing and devolving, as well as securitizing immigration have all been identified as key markers of the growing neo-liberalization of immigration policy at the national level in Canada" (Dobrowolsky 2013, 198). As in the United States, the immigration policy is divided into immigration control policy and immigrant integration policy. Immigration control policy is in the hands of the federal government like in the majority of the countries worldwide.

Boushey and Luedtke (2006) describe the immigration policy area as "concurrent power" in the Canadian Constitution, "meaning that jurisdiction is formally shared between Ottawa and the provinces." The Canadian provinces are allowed to make immigration laws, possessing greater power in integration and resettlement processes than the federal government for more than 100 years. However, Barker (2015) argues that the federal government still controls refugee and family reunification and temporary migrant categories.

The immigration integration system is regionalized. Each province has a separate agreement with the federal government, due to the differences in demographics, and social and economic opportunities for immigrants in communities (Leo and August 2009). On the other hand, Canada is witness to a high level of "marketization" of immigration policy at a subnational level "market-oriented approach that is blind to the relevance of the social will not meet governments' economic or demographic, social, or political objectives" (Dobrowolsky 2013, 216). All ten provinces are engaged in re-settlement and integration practices. However, Montreal, Vancouver, and Toronto are three metropolitan areas that account for 80 percent of the foreign-born population. These areas, which are accordingly located in Quebec, British Columbia, and Toronto provinces, attract the most attention from the federal, state, and nonprofit organizations (Schmidt 2007).

As immigration policy and programs are decentralized, the federal government is more distant from local affairs in communities and, thus, has fewer partnerships with nonprofit organizations than provincial and local governments. According to Biles (2008), in 2005 the federal government had only twenty-one contribution agreements with over 300 civil society organizations, which deliver integration services. Provinces and local stakeholders have ultimate responsibility for the actual implementation of settlement and integration programs.

In 2008, Citizenship and Immigration Canada (CIC) launched Local Immigration Partnerships (LIPs), an innovative initiative that established the key role of community-based partnership and planning in immigrant settlement services. LIPs is a mechanism through which CIC supports the development of community-based partnerships and planning around the needs of newcomers. LIPs establish broad-based coordinating councils that engage a variety of stakeholders and key community leaders from different sectors in a locally-driven strategic planning process (Citizenship and Immigration Canada 2013).

According to the initiative the following actors are key to the process (CIC 2013, 11):

- Local civil society organizations;
- Municipal representatives (transit, housing, libraries, recreation and culture, police, social services);
- Provincial/territorial representatives (immigration, health, justice, education and training, housing, school boards, regional economic development agencies);
- Federal Representatives (CIC, HRSDC, Service Canada, PHAC, Agriculture and Agri-food Canada (Rural and Co-operatives Secretariat), economic development agencies);
- Labor Market Actors (Employers, training boards, business councils/associations, chambers of commerce and unions);
- Umbrella Organizations (United Way, YMCA, Boys and Girls Clubs);
- Media (Mainstream and Ethnic Local and Regional Research Bodies).

According to Evans and Shields (2014), co-governance requires not only coproduction of services between nonprofit and governmental agencies. New Public Governance also recognizes the advocacy role of civil society organizations. NPG promotes collaborative network governance approach, where involved stakeholders partner interdependently and horizontally. Evans and Shields (2014) show that Canadian local governments do not show high intent in seeking nonprofits' advice in shaping immigration policies. At the same time, open communications between nonprofit-government are important for both the government, which receives information about immigrant communities, and nonprofits, which help to shape their programs. On the contrary, Leo and August (2009) show that there is evidence of a positive impact of partnerships with community groups on immigrant integration programming. In 2010 Ontario Liberal government launched a Partnership Project that "promoted cooperative relationships with the nonprofit sector, based on mutual respect and more flexible and sustaining partnering with nonprofit providers" (Evan and Shields 2014, 123).

The Canadian immigration system consists of some rudiments of New Public Governance. Still, the federal and provincial contract-funding regime impedes the development of more progressive, collaborative models of immigrant integration service delivery. As in the United States, nonprofits' desire to be actively engaged in immigrant advocacy is being restricted by the dependence on federal and provincial funding. Nonprofits are more engaged in competitive bidding rather than in coproduction of immigrant settlement services with government agencies. Public agencies see nongovernmental organizations more as community advocates and advisors, rather than equal partners in service delivery. However, several local and national initiatives, such as LIP, show that the collaborative process is gradually emerging and developing.

The Case of Mexico

The immigration system in Mexico has often been criticized for violations of human rights and high rates of deportation of undocumented immigrants (Michel 2002). At the same time, Mexico demands openness for its emigrants in neighboring countries, the United States and Canada (González-Murphy and Koslowski 2011).

The immigration system is centralized. The federal government has authority to enact laws over both immigration control policy and immigrant integration policy, by controlling and enforcing laws through Mexico's National Institute of Migration (INM) and Mexico's Ministry of the Interior (SEGOB) (Michel 2002). The General Law of Population of 1974 with its regulations serve as the main migration policy, the main objective of which is to "to regulate phenomena affecting the population, regarding its volume, structure, dynamics, and distribution in the national territory, in order to achieve its just and equitable participation in the benefits of the social and economic development" (González-Murphy and Koslowski 2011, 4).

Mexican federal, state, and local authorities are required to request proof of lawful immigration status from foreigners appearing before them. In this way, Mexico keeps track of everyone who is within its borders. Illegal immigrants are deported or prosecuted. According to Article 188, foreigners who attempt to reenter the country after being deported can be imprisoned up to ten years (González-Muprhy and Koslowski 2011).

Although the migration system in Mexico is considered to be highly centralized and strict, Mexican federal and local governments, together with academicians and civil society members, have made several collaborative attempts to develop a proposal for migration policy reform. In 2005, the report Towards a Migration Policy for the Mexican State had been enacted by INM and presented to the United States government. The countries agreed upon the 15-20-year revision of the policy.

Nevertheless, there have been some remarkably positive moments in establishing nonprofit-government relations for immigrant integration in Mexico. In order to improve its image, Mexico proposed acceptance and integration of Guatemalan and El Salvadoran refugees (Michel 2002; González-Murphy and Koslowski 2011). Sin Fronteras is a nongovernmental organization founded in 1995. Initially, the organization aimed to advocate for immigrants' rights. Currently, the organization provides direct services to refugees and immigrants in education, job training, healthcare, and housing. The nonprofit also oversees migration centers across Mexico. "In a collaborative effort with the state, it offers workshops aimed at educating immigration officials on human rights issues" (González-Murphy and Valeria 2009). The organization receives its funds mostly from the United Nations High Commissioner for Refugees (UNHCR) as well as American based foundations, such as MacArthur Foundation and Ford Foundation (Sin Fronteras 2017).

Three faith-based Catholic organizations, COMI, Casas del Migrante, and Pastoral de Movilidad Humana and its Hermanos en el Camino Shelter, address first needs of immigrants and refugees, such as housing, clothing, and legal assistance. Although these organizations are a part of larger networks that share information about immigrants, their shelters work independently from each other. If any of these organizations observe that human rights of migrants are violated, they submit a request for *collaboration* to the federal government (González-Murphy and Valeria 2009, 258). González-Murphy

(2009) confirms that networks and regular contacts between the federal government and civil society organizations do exist. However, they are concealed by the government website.

In the case of Mexico, where immigration policies are centralized, civil society organizations play a crucial role as autonomous service providers or advocacy groups in providing services independently from government. Nongovernmental organizations receive most of their funding from private foundations inside and outside Mexico. Financially stronger organizations facilitate some collaboration and cooperation with the federal government in matters such as human rights advocacy. However, the majority of nonprofits have limited resources and capacities, which take a lot of their effort to focus on providing services, rather than on influencing policy.

This is confounded by the overall low levels of civic participation, particularly among the poor in Mexican society. Ironically, the poor in Mexican society were some of the most active in mobilizing to support democratization, and yet now they are the least engaged in public affairs and civic life. In the old regime, the poor were engaged through targeted mobilization by elite power holders, who permitted such activism to support broader political aims; now, without such marshaled or manipulated mobilization, the poor are not engaged, except in helping neighbors within their communities. This is an act independent of politics or the state (Holzner 2010).

Poor participation, or participation of the poor, is significant in thinking about implications for refugee and migrant management and integration. For instance, if there is to be competition for low/no-skill jobs from newcomers to society, the poor are key stakeholders for involvement. This is not the case, however, and so decentralization and engagement of civil society in migration and refugee policies is constrained. The broader democratic implication from a war on poverty and war on impoverished citizenship perspective is cleanly stated as such: "[T]he voice of the poor in Mexico is heard neither loudly nor clearly, and certainly not equally, impoverishing democracy as a result" (Holzner 2010, 215). This "participation gap" threatens democratic institutions the world over (Dalton 2017).

Organizing the Power Structure Summary

Canada has decentralized immigrant integration policies and redistribution of power and authority to provinces and municipalities in enacting laws and managing migration. However, the use of tools of governance is just emerging in the immigration policy area. The new program LIP initiated by the federal government gives an impetus for collaborative practices in communities, by bringing local stakeholders from all sectors, and officials from all levels of government together for strategic planning to address the needs of newcomers. However, it is too early to analyze successes or failures of the use of new governance tools in Canadian communities.

In the case of Mexico, due to the country's early transition to democracy and highly centralized immigration policies, nonprofit organizations exist as strategic competitors, advocates, and autonomous service providers. The majority of nonprofits, which provide settlement services, work independently from government, receiving their funds mostly from the larger international nongovernmental organizations or from foundations in the United States. However, in response to worldwide criticism, the federal government showed some attempt in developing a new immigration system by bringing different stakeholders, politicians, academicians, and civil society leaders together in a process of collaborative policymaking. By gaining support from international stakeholders, the local organizations in Mexico engage in even more advocacy for immigrants, compared to local civil society organizations in the United States and Canada, which rely mostly on government grants.

Global Comparative Summary

Comparison across countries on questions such as civics and poverty can have several benefits (Bryer and Medina 2017, 522): "(1) comparing like or unlike cases can generate new theoretical insight about social phenomena, (2) comparison can serve to inspire innovative action to achieve desirable social or societal aims, and (3) comparison can help organizational and government leaders to understand not only what works but also where failure may be occurring, thus allowing for improved practice." These are the aims of the brief comparative cases presented in this chapter.

The comparisons herein are diverse, addressing different aspects of poverty and civics. They each are worthy of more robust analysis on their own, and relevant citations are provided to guide the reader to such broader and more detailed treatments of these subjects. Most compellingly these comparisons suggest where some of the ideas presented in previous chapters might fit and where those ideas might be improved.

First, we can suggest that all societies that have been subject to comparison endure (or promote or provoke) the same challenges as found in the United States. Poor citizens are not fully included-in legally (through restriction), politically and ethically (through credibility of participation), or culturally or religiously (through opportunities for free expression). Some societies are more "tolerant" than others, but the tendency to create and maintain an "other" and to align that otherness with the conditions of living in poverty span societies. Adding refugees to the mix exacerbates these tensions, particularly if it is assumed that many refugees are lacking desirable skills and values of life (i.e., that they are poor).

Second, we can identify notable efforts to achieve victory in some of the battles, as described in the seventh chapter, namely expertise versus mass competence, and so on (see table 7.1). Strategies of mobilization, cooptation, persuasion, and exclusion are used to varying degrees across comparison countries, sometimes by choice and sometimes based on resource constraints. Indeed, it may be necessary, for instance, in Lithuanian society to further develop civil society organizations and promote a certain amount of cooperation (insiders to outsiders) in order to reach further into society and build trust across the broader citizenry. In the Netherlands and United States, by comparison, perhaps we have more opportunity through already relatively strong civil societies to empower the people directly without a broker agency standing as potentially unaccountable representative (as per the fourth chapter).

That all societies are unique and will require equally unique resources to achieve victory in the wars on poverty and impoverished citizenship, to solve the democratic dilemma of empowerment without manipulation, is perhaps a simple statement and fully expected in any of the social sciences. The solution depends. However, certain core values, we suggest, can stand firmly across contexts. We conclude with discussion of this potential tension and other themes that have emerged throughout this text.

~

Conclusion

Throughout the world, though we approach the questions of democracy and government-citizen relationship from unique cultural and historical perspectives, we share a commitment to learning what can work best to build relationships that address our most challenging problems. Poverty is one such problem; perhaps it is time to renew a call to arms for both a war on poverty and war on impoverished citizenship. In the previous chapters, we considered the state of poverty and poor citizenship in the United States and in comparison to other nations around the world, identified battlefronts for turning the tide for combatting these issues, and suggested possible pathways forward to wage a new war and win it.

This is all written within the context of a global political landscape that is fast shifting: the British are entering what will be a challenging few years as they negotiate the terms of divorce from the European Union; the Americans in 2016 elected a president driven forward, despite expectations, by populist winds; political turmoil threatens moderate voices on issues of immigration and poverty in both of these countries, as well as others, including Hungary and Poland. Open threats to the ruling classes are causing observers of global politics and culture to ask what is changing in the world and seeking explanation. We see unexpected political headlines and social movements emerge in France and the Netherlands; we see political scandal wreak havoc in places such as Brazil, South Korea, and Israel; and, we see democracies or the faint glimmers of democracy falter in places like Turkey, Egypt, Poland, and Venezuela.

We are living today in a world defined in a similar way as the 1st century Roman Empire. A character in the historical fiction novel, *Captivity*, by Hungarian novelist, Gyorgy Spiro, says: "Quite likely what is actually happening on earth is not that which we see happening, but *something* is quite definitely happening right now, even though it's possible we shall never get to know the truth of the age during which we sojourned." These words can be spoken as truly about the political, social, and cultural shifts that are occurring in the increasingly interconnected world in which we, by the circumstances of fate, find ourselves living.

In such periods of human history, when change is afoot, we as individuals and as part of collectives, can choose, within limits, to allow change to occur without or despite us. Alternatively, we can, at least within our small corners of the world, drive the change. With respect to poverty, the choice is the same. Here, though, is the democratic dilemma. To take control of our personal history in our individual lives, and/or take control of our fleeting second of human history, requires empowerment, as the systemic issues that have made poverty a permanent societal fixture are rigid (Royce 2015).

It requires empowerment of the poor and non-poor to at once claim their individuality and exercise their power as a mass. As we considered in the fourth chapter, the non-poor included-in citizens have control over their individuality but are controlled by social norms and pressures to belong within the politically powerful "middle class"; the poor included-out citizens have little control over their individuality and have no political power as a mass. Non-poor must reclaim their individuality, and poor must develop the power of their group without alienating the non-poor and while demonstrating their individual attributes outside the group.

To fight the wars on poverty and impoverished citizenship, then, requires considerably more than government policies and programs that give access to material resources. Poverty is more than subsistence poverty, and other forms of poverty exacerbate subsistence poverty. To fight these wars requires a marshaling and leveraging of all bureaucratic resources of governments across levels, and a leveraging of financial, intellectual, emotional, and human resources available across sectors.

The power structure as it exists today must be organized, expanded, and assisted simultaneously, and confronted only with caution and without manipulation of the poor from outside. A lesson from community action agencies in the 1960s is that confrontation makes the powerful nervous, and the included-in and powerful can keep those engaging in confrontation out. They can withstand the struggle, most especially when the pawns in the struggle are not empowered to act on their own and do not have the capacity to hold their handlers to account for decisions. Confrontation is necessary, but the ground troops must have full agency in their actions and genuine empowerment expressed through their words.

To win a war on poverty requires transformation not only of economic systems, as Oxfam (2017) emphasizes but of social and cultural systems. These are not changes that can be controlled from above; for the changes to take hold, and to enable genuine empowerment, there must be an introduction of multiple programs and initiatives aimed in the same direction. To use the war metaphor, this is not an air war with drone technology; we must get our hands dirty in direct combat, in each and every community, block, business, and home. The kinds of initiatives suggested in the seventh chapter are possible examples of the kinds of battle plans that can be utilized at these different levels of society.

Suggestions in chapter 7 can potentially alter the course in battling subsistence, agency, and status poverties simultaneously; there are other initiatives and micro-changes to bureaucratic procedure or use of emergent social technologies, for instance, that can allow for effective combat against status or agency poverties alone, without addressing subsistence poverty at the same time. For instance, we can see novel ideas emerging from scholars, activists, and politicians such as: Tina Nabatchi and Matt Leighninger (2015) writing about deliberative democracy and public participation; Jeffrey Hou (2010) and Howard Gillette (2010) writing about urban planning and its linkage to citizenship; Gavin Newsom and Lisa Dickey (2013) and Wael Ghonim (2012) writing about using emergent social technologies to engage citizens; Alan Khazei (2010) writing on volunteerism; and, M. V. Lee Badgett (2015) and Patrick Blessinger and John Anchan (2015) writing on the role of higher education institutions in promoting citizenship in all of its forms.

To fight these wars, we need to marshal all these resources, one block at a time, if necessary, but with leveraging power of our governments to incentivize change. These are values that can cross contexts, whereas the specific interventions can and will vary given unique political contexts and historical legacies. Through these tools, though, we can achieve participation of the poor and enhance poor participation of all . . . towards Maximum Empowerment Participation and a war that is won by the people, not by the government and not by poverty.

References

Abdel-Magied, Yassmin. "What Does My Headscarf Mean to You?" *TED*, 27 May 2015. Web. 28 Oct. 2017.

Ackerman, Bruce, Anne Alstott, and Philippe Van Parij. *Redesigning Distribution: Basic Income and Stakeholder Grants as Alternative Cornerstones for a More Egalitarian Capitalism*. Brooklyn: Verso Books, 2006. Print.

Adams, Guy B., and Danny L. Balfour. *Unmasking Administrative Evil*. Armonk: M. E. Sharpe, 2004.

Alcindor, Yamiche. "Comments on Poverty Start Uproar." *The New York Times*, 25 May 2017. Web. 25 May 2017.

Alinsky, Saul. *Rules for Radicals: A Practical Primer for Realistic Radicals*. New York: Vintage Books, 1989.

Allard, Scott W. *Places in Need: The Changing Geography of Poverty*. New York: Russell Sage Foundation, 2017.

Arnstein, Sherry R. "A Ladder of Citizen Participation." *Journal of the American Institute of Planners* 35.4 (1969): 216–24.

Attar, Beth K., Nancy G. Guerra, and Patrick H. Tolan. 1994. "Neighborhood Disadvantage, Stressful Life Events and Adjustments in Urban Elementary-School Children." *Journal of Clinical Child Psychology* 23.4 (1994): 391–400.

Badgett, M. V. Lee. *The Public Professor: How to Use Your Research to Change the World*. New York: New York University Press, 2015.

Baker, William H., H. Lon Addams, and Brian Davis. "Critical Factors for Enhancing Municipal Public Hearings." *Public Administration Review* 65.4 (2005): 490–99.

Bane, Mary Jo. "Poverty Politics and Policy." *Focus*, Madison: University of Wisconsin-Madison Institute for Research on Poverty (2009): 75–80.

Bannink, Duco, and Ringo Ossewaarde. "Decentralization: New Modes of Governance and Administrative Responsibility." *Administration & Society* 44.5 (2012): 595–624.

Barker, Fiona. *Nationalism, Identity and the Governance of Diversity: Old Politics, New Arrivals.* New York: Springer, 2015.

Barnhoorn, Florie. "The Netherlands: All That's Left is the Action: Where Do We Stand with the Experiments?" *Basic Income Earth Network*, Basic Income Earth Network, n.d. 12 Aug. 2017.

Basic Income Earth Network. "What is Unconditional Basic Income?" *Basic Income Earth Network*, Basic Income Earth Network, n.d. 12 Aug. 2017.

Berry, Jeffrey, Kent E. Portney, and Ken Thomson. *The Rebirth of Urban Democracy.* Washington, DC: Brookings Institution Press, 1993.

Bielefeld, Wolfgang, and William Suhs Cleveland. "Faith-based Organizations as Service Providers and Their Relationship to Government." *Nonprofit and Voluntary Sector Quarterly* 42.3 (2013): 468–94.

Bierbaum, Mira, and Franziska Gassmann. "Limits of Freedom? Experienes with the Participation Act." *Policy Brief*, United Nations University, 2016.

Biles, John. "Integration Policies in English-Speaking Canada." *Immigration and Integration in Canada in the Twenty-first Century* (2008): 139–86.

Blessinger, Patrick, and John P. Anchan. *Democratizing Higher Education: International Comparative Perspectives.* New York: Routledge, 2015.

Bloch, Hannah. "That Little Syrian Boy: Here's Who He Was." *National Public Radio Morning Edition*, 3 Sept. 2015. Web. 2015.

Bloom, Paul. *Against Empathy: The Case for Rational Compassion.* New York: HarperCollins, 2016.

Borgatti, Stephen P., and Pacey C. Foster. "The Network Paradigm in Organizational Research: A Review and Typology." *Journal of Management* 29.6 (2003): 991–1013.

Boushey, Graeme, and Adam Luedtke. "Fiscal Federalism and the Politics of Immigration: Centralized and Decentralized Immigration Policies in Canada and the United States." *Journal of Comparative Policy Analysis* 8.3 (2006): 207–24.

Bousquet, Steve. "Thousands of Florida Felons Wait Decades to Regain the Right to Vote." *Miami Herald*, 13 July 2017. Web. 13 July 2017.

Brady, David, and Rebekah Burroway. "Targeting, Universalism, and Single-Mother Poverty: A Multilevel Analysis Across 18 Affluent Democracies." *Demography* 49 (2012): 719–46.

Bretherton, Luke. *Resurrecting Democracy: Faith, Citizenship, and the Politics of a Common Life.* Cambridge: Cambridge University Press, 2015.

Broder, David S. *Democracy Derailed: Initiative Campaigns and the Power of Money.* New York: Harcourt, 2000.

Brooks, David. "How We are Ruining America." *The New York Times*, 11 July 2017. Web. 11 July 2017.

Brown, Anastasia, and Todd Scribner. "Unfulfilled Promises, Future Possibilities: The Refugee Resettlement System in the United States." *Journal on Migration & Hum. Security* 2 (2014): 101.

Bryer, Thomas A. "Toward a Relevant Agenda for a Responsive Public Administration." *Journal of Public Adminsitration Research and Theory* 17.3 (2007): 479–500.

———. "Living Democracy in Theory and Practice: Getting Dirty in a Local Government Incorporation Process." *Public Administration and Management* 15.1 (2010): 259–304.

———. "Online Public Engagement in the Obama Administration: Building a Democracy Bubble?" *Police & Internet* 3.4 (2011): Article 3.

———. "The Costs of Democratization: Social Media Adaptation Challenges within Government Agencies." *Administrative Theory & Praxis* 33.3 (2011b): 341–61.

———. "Identity Crisis: Searching for Personal Responsibility, Justice, and Community in the Real Estate Market Crash." *Public Integrity* 14.3 (2012): 299–311.

———. "Encouraging Citizenship in U.S. Presidential Administrations: An Analysis of Presidential Records." *The State of Citizen Participation in America*, Ed. Hindy Schachter and Kaifeng Yang. Charlotte: Information Age Publishing, 2012b. 55–75.

———. "Public Participation in Regulatory Decision-Making: Cases from Regulations.gov." *Public Performance and Management Review* 37.2 (2013): 263–79.

———. *Higher Education Beyond Job Creation: Universities, Citizenship, and Community*. Lanham: Lexington Books, 2014.

———. "Together for Tomorrow: Improving Title I Education through Inter-Sectoral and Governmental Collaboration." *Journal of Public Management and Social Policy* 20.1 (2014b): 29–46.

———. *National Service and Volunteerism: Achieving Impact in Our Communities*. Lanham: Lexington Books, 2015.

Bryer, Thomas A., and Terry L. Cooper. "George Frederickson and the Dialogue on Citizenship in Public Administration." *Public Administration Review* 72.s (2012): s108–s15.

Bryer, Thomas A., and Pamela Medina. "Global Perspectives on Civic Health: Applying Lessons from Post-Community Societies to Enable Greater Civic Outcomes in the United States." *Journal of Health and Human Services* 39.4 (2017): 520–42.

Bryer, Thomas A., and Ismael Sahin. "Administrators as Deliberative Representatives: A Revised Public Service Role." *International Journal of Public Administration* 35.14 (2012): 925–33.

Bryer, Thomas A., Maria-Elena Augustin, and Emily Bachman. "Three Sectors and a University: The Creation of a High Impact AmeriCorps VISTA Project." *National Service and Volunteerism: Achieving Impact in Our Communities*, Ed. Thomas A. Bryer. Lanham: Lexington Books, 2015. 19–24.

Bryer, Thomas A., Maria-Elena Augustin, Mukta Barve, Norma Gracia, and Valerie Perez. "Fighting Poverty with Passion and a University Partner: The Creation of a High Impact AmeriCorps VISTA Program." *Journal of Nonprofit Management* 16.1 (2013): 46–60.

Bunch, Beverly S., and Dalitso S. Sulamoyo. *Community Action Leadership: Rooting Out Poverty at the Local Level.* New York: Routledge, 2017.

Burghardt, John, Peter Z. Schochet, Sheena McConnell, Terry Johnson, R. Mark Gritz, Steven Glazerman, John Homrighausen, and Russell Jackson. "Does Job Corps Work? Summary of the National Job Corps Study." Document No. PR01-50. Princeton, NJ: Mathematica Policy Research, Inc., 2017.

Burtless, Gary, and Timothy M. Smeeding. "Poverty, Work, and Policy: The United States in Comparative Perspective." Testimony prepared for the Subcommittee on Income Security and Family Support, Committee on Ways and Means, Congress of the United States, 13 Feb. 2007.

Butkeviciene, Egle, Thomas A. Bryer, Egle Vaidelyte, and Vaidas Morkevicius. "Differentiating Online and Offline Political Participation in Eastern and Western Europe: Implications for New Public Governance." *Public Performance and Management Review*, In press.

Cacho, Lisa Marie. *Social Death: Racialized Rightlessness and the Criminalization of the Unprotected.* New York: New York University Press, 2012.

Casper, Barry M. *Lost in Washington: Finding the Way Back to Democracy in America.* Boston: University of Massachusetts Press, 2000.

Cazenave, Noel A. *Impossible Democracy: The Unlikely Success of the War on Poverty Community Action Programs.* Albany: State University of New York Press, 2007.

Center for Budget and Policy Priorities. "Policy Basics: An Introduction to TANF." *Center for Budget and Policy Priorities*, 2015. Web. 12 Aug. 2017.

———. "Policy Basics: The Housing Choice Voucher Program." *Center for Budget and Policy Priorities*, 2017. Web. 12 Aug. 2017.

Chase, Elaine, and Robert Walker. "The Co-construction of Shame in the Context of Poverty: Beyond a Threat to the Social Bond." *Sociology* 47.4 (2012): 739–54.

Chomsky, Aviva. *"They Take Our Jobs!" and 20 Other Myths About Immigration.* Boston: Beacon Press, 2007.

Ci, Jiwei. "Agency and Other Stakes of Poverty." *The Journal of Political Philosophy* 21.2 (2013): 125–50.

Citizenship and Immigration Canada. Local Immigration Partnerships Handbook, 2013.

Clifford, Stephanie, and Jessica Silver-Greenberg. "Foster Care as Punishment: The New Reality of 'Jane Crow.'" *The New York Times*, 23 July 2017. Web. 23 July 2017.

Cohen, Patricia. "On Health and Welfare, Moral Arguments Can Outweigh Economics." *The New York Times*, 7 May 2017. Web. 7 May 2017.

Cooper, Terry L. "The Hidden Price Tag: Participation Costs and Health Planning." *American Journal of Public Health* 69.4 (1979): 368–74.

——. *An Ethic of Citizenship for Public Administration*. Englewood Cliffs: Prentice Hall, 1991.

Cooper, Terry L., Thomas A. Bryer, and Jack W. Meek. "Citizen-Centered Collaborative Public Management." *Public Administration Review* 66.Special Issue (2006): 76–88.

Cove, Peter. *Poor No More: Rethinking Dependency and the War on Poverty*. New Brunswick: Transaction Publishers, 2017.

Crenson, Matthew A., and Benjamin Ginsberg. *Downsizing Democracy: How America Sidelined its Citizens and Privatized its Public*. Baltimore: Johns Hopkins University Press, 2002.

Cunha, Darlena. "This is What Happened When I Drove my Mercedes to Pick Up Food Stamps." *The Washington Post*, 8 July 2014. Web. 12 Aug. 2017.

Currid-Halkett, Elizabeth. *The Sum of Small Things: A Theory of the Aspirational Class*. Princeton: Princeton University Press, 2017.

d'Toqueville, Alexis. *Democracy in America*. Trans. Harvey C. Mansfield and Delba Winthrop. Chicago: University of Chicago Press, 2000[1840].

Dalton, Russell J. *The Participation Gap: Social Status and Political Inequality*. Oxford: Oxford University Press, 2017.

Dalton, Russell J., and Christian Welzel. *The Civic Culture Transformed: From Allegiant to Assertive Citizens*. Cambridge: Cambridge University Press, 2014.

Delgado, Richard, and Jean Stefancic. *Critical Race Theory: An Introduction*. New York: New York University Press, 2017.

Denhardt, Janet V., and Robert D. Denhardt. *The New Public Service: Serving, Not Steering*. New York: Routledge, 2015.

Dewey, Caitlin, and Tracy Jan. "Trump's Plans to Cut Food Stamps Could Hit His Supporters Hardest." *The Washington Post*, 22 May 2017. Web. 22 May 2017.

Dobrowolsky, Alexandra. "Nuancing Neoliberalism: Lessons Learned from a Failed Immigration Experiment." *Journal of International Migration and Integration* 14.2 (2013): 197–218.

Downie, Elaine. "Nothing About Us, Without Us, is For Us!" *SCVO*. 5 Sep. 2016. Web. 15 Aug. 2017.

Dreier, Peter, John Mollenkopf, and Todd Swanstrom. *Place Matters: Metropolitis for the Twenty-first Century*. Lawrence: University of Kansas Press, 2014.

Durkheim, Emile. *Socialism*. Forgotten Books, 2012.

Dvorak, Jaroslav. "Lithuania." *The SAGE Encyclopedia of World Poverty*. Thousand Oaks: SAGE Publications, 2015. 920–21.

Easterly, William. *The Tyranny of Experts: Economists, Dictators, and the Forgotten Rights of the Poor*. New York: Basic Books, 2013.

Edwards, Keith E., and David A. McKelfresh. "The Impact of a Living Learning Center on Students' Academic Success and Persistence." *Journal of College Student Development* 43.3 (2002): 395–402.

Eikenberry, Angela M. *Giving Circles: Philanthropy, Voluntary Association, and Democracy*. Bloomington: Indiana University Press, 2009.

Eisenstadt, Shmuel N. "Transformation of Social Political, and Cultural Orders in Modernization." *American Sociological Review* (1965): 659–73.

Elmelech, Yuval, and Hsien-Hen Lu. "Race, Ethnicity, and the Gender Poverty Gap." *Social Science Research* 33.1 (2004): 158–82.

Erni, John Nguyet. "Citizenship Management: On the Politics of Being Included-Out." *International Journal of Cultural Studies* 19.3 (2016): 323–40.

Espiritu, Yen Le. *Home Bound: Filipino American Lives across Cultures, Communities, and Countries*. Berkeley: University of California Press, 2003.

Etzioni, Amitai. *Spirit of Community*. New York: Simon and Schuster, 1994.

Evans, Bryan, and John Shields. "Nonprofit Engagement with Provincial Policy Officials: The Case of NGO Policy Voice in Canadian Immigrant Settlement Services." *Policy and Society* 33.2 (2014): 117–27.

Farazmand, Ali. "Bureaucracy and Democracy: A Theoretical Analysis." *Public Organization Review* 10.3 (2010): 245–58.

Feiock, Richard C., and Simon A. Andrew. "Introduction: Understanding the Relationships Between Nonprofit Organizations and Local Governments." *International Journal of Public Administration* 29.10–11 (2006): 759–67.

Ferragina, Emanuele, Mark Tomlinson, and Robert Walker. *Poverty, Participation and Choice: The Legacy of Peter Townsend*. Joseph Rowntree Foundation, 2013.

Fink, Leon. *Progressive Intellectuals and the Dilemmas of Democratic Commitment*. Cambridge: Harvard University Press, 1997.

Fisher, Gordon M. "The Development and History of the Poverty Thresholds." *Social Security Bulletin* 55.3 (1992).

Fjellberg, Anders. "Two Nameless Bodies Washed Up on the Beach. Here are Their Stories." *TED*. 2014. Web. 11 Aug. 2017.

Flathman, Richard. "Citizenship and Authority: A Chastened View of Citizenship." *News for Teachers of Political Science* 30 (1981): 9–19.

Follett, Mary Parker. *The New State: Group Organization the Solution of Popular Government*. Penn State Press, 1918.

Fosler, R. Scott. 2002. *Working Better Together: How Government, Business, and Nonprofit Organizations Can Achieve Public Purposes Through Cross-Sector Collaboration, Alliances, and Partnerships*, 2002.

Fox, Liana, Christopher Wimer, Irwin Garfinkel, Neeraj Kaushal, Jaehyun Nam, and Jane Waldfogel. *Trends in Deep Poverty from 1968 to 2011: The Influence of Family Structure, Employment Patterns, and the Safety Net*. Russell Sage Foundation, 2015.

Freire, Paulo. *Pedagogy of the Oppressed*. New York: Continuum, 2011.

Frontline. "Poverty, Politics, and Profit." Public Broadcasting System. 9 May 2017. Web. 12 Aug. 2017.

Fry, Brian R. *Mastering Public Administration*. Chatham, 1989.

Gans, Herbert. *The War Against the Poor: The Underclass and Antipoverty Policy*. Basic Books, 1995.

Gazley, Beth. "Beyond the Contract: The Scope and Nature of Informal Government–Nonprofit Partnerships." *Public Administration Review* 68.1 (2008): 141–54.

Gazley, Beth, and Jeffrey L. Brudney. "The Purpose (and Perils) of Government-Nonprofit Partnership." *Nonprofit and Voluntary Sector Quarterly* 36.3 (2007): 389–415.

Ghonim, Wael. *Revolution 2.0: The Power of the People is Greater than the People in Power*. Boston: Houghton Mifflin Harcourt, 2012.

Gidron, Benjamin, Ralph M. Kramer, and Lester M. Salamon. *Government and the Third Sector: Emerging Relationships in Welfare States*. San Francisco: Jossey-Bass, 1992.

Gillette Jr., Howard. *Civitas By Design: Building Better Communities, from the Garden City to the New Urbanism*. Philadelphia: University of Pennsylvania Press, 2010.

Gillette, Michael L. *Launching the War on Poverty: An Oral History*. Oxford: Oxford University Press, 2010.

Gillezeau, Rob. "Did the War on Poverty Cause Race Riots?" 2010. Web. 24 Oct. 2017.

Giordani, Paolo E., and Michele Ruta. "The Immigration Policy Puzzle." *Review of International Economics* 19.5 (2011): 922–35.

Goldfield, David R. "Black Political Power and Public Policy in the Urban South." *Urban Policy in Twentieth-Century America*, 1993.

González-Murphy, and Laura Valeria. *Change and Continuity in Mexico's Immigration Policy: How Civil Society Organizations Influence the Policy Process*. State University of New York at Albany, 2009.

González-Murphy, Laura Valeria, and Rey Koslowski. "Understanding Mexico's Changing Immigration Laws." *Woodrow Wilson International Center for Scholars*. 2011. Web. 24 Oct. 2017.

Goodin, Robert E., and Julian Le Grand. "Creeping Universalism in the Australian Welfare State." *Not Only the Poor*. London: Allen and Unwin, 1987.

Green, Erica L. "Trump's Plan to Cut National Service Programs Breaks Decades of Tradition." *The New York Times*, 2017. Web. 26 May 2017.

Gunnar, Megan R., Kristin Frenn, Sandi S. Wewerka, and Mark J. Van Ryzin. "Moderate versus Severe Early Life Stress: Associations with Stress Reactivity and Regulation in 10–12-Year-Old Children." *Psychoneuroendocrinology* 34.1 (2009): 62–75.

Harlem Children's Zone. "About Us." 2017 Web. 12 Aug. 2017.

———. 2017b. "Our Results." 2017b. Web. 12 Aug. 2017.

Haskins, Ron. "Poverty and Opportunity: Begin with Facts." Testimony before Congress of the United States. January 28, 2014.

Hepburn, Eve, and Ricard Zapata-Barrero. *The Politics of Immigration in Multi-Level States: Governance and Political Parties*. New York: Springer, 2014.

Herranz Jr., Joaquin. "The Multisectoral Trilemma of Network Management." *Journal of Public Administration Research and Theory* 18.1 (2007): 1–31.

HighScope. "Perry Preschool Study." 2017. Web. 12 Aug. 2017.

Hirsch, Arnold Richard, and Raymond A. Mohl. *Urban Policy in Twentieth-Century America*. Camden: Rutgers University Press, 1993.

Holzner, Claudio A. *Poverty of Democracy: The Institutional Roots of Political Participation in Mexico*. Pittsburgh: University of Pittsburgh Press, 2010.

Hood, Christopher. "A Public Management for All Seasons?" *Public Administration* 69.1 (1991): 3–19.

Hou, Jeffrey. *Insurgent Public Space: Guerrilla Urbanism and the Remaking of Contemporary Cities*. New York: Routledge, 2010.

Hungerford, Thomas L., and Rebecca Thiess. "The Earned Income Tax Credit and the Child Tax Credit: History Purpose, Goals, and Effectiveness." *Issue Brief #370*, Economic Policy Institute, 2013.

Huttenlocher, Janellen. "Language Input and Language Growth." *Preventive Medicine* 27.2 (1998): 195–99.

Iceland, John. *Poverty in America: A Handbook*. Berkeley: University of California Press, 2012.

Independent Staff. "Finland's Universal Basic Income Trial for Unemployed Reduces Stress Levels, Says Officials." *The Independent*, 8 May 2017. Web. 12 Aug. 2017.

Inkelas, Karen K., and Jennifer L. Weisman. "Different by Design: An Examination of Student Outcomes among Participants in Three Types of Living-Learning Programs." *Journal of College Student Development* 44.3 (2003): 335–68.

Ipsos. "Public Perspectives: Universal Basic Income." Ipsos. 2017. Web 12 Aug. 2017.

Izaguirre, Anthony. "For Homeless on Heroin, Treatment Can Be Elusive with No ID." Associated Press, 4 Aug. 2017. Web. 4 Aug. 2017.

Jackson-Elmoore, Cynthia, Richard C. Hula, and Laura A. Reese. 2011. *Reinventing Civil Society: The Emerging Role of Faith-Based Organizations*. Armonk: M. E. Sharpe.

Jensen, Eric. *Teaching with Poverty in Mind: What Being Poor Does to Kids' Brains and What Schools Can Do About It*. Alexandria: ACSD, 2009.

Kalu, Kalu N. *Citizenship: Identity, Institutions and the Postmodern Challenge*. New York: Routledge, 2017.

Katz, Michael B. *In the Shadow of the Poorhouse: A Social History of Welfare in America*. New York: Basic Books, 1996.

———. *The Undeserving Poor: America's Enduring Confrontation with Poverty*. Oxford: Oxford University Press, 2013.

Kennedy, Robert F. *Statement of the Honorable Robert F. Kennedy, Attorney General of the United States, before the House Committee on Education and Labor, in Support of H.R. 10440, the Economic Opportunity Act of 1964*, 1964.

Khazei, Alan. *Big Citizenship: How Pragmatic Idealism can Bring Out the Best in America*. New York: PublicAffairs, 2010.

Kneebone, Elizabeth, and Alan Berube. *Confronting Suburban Poverty in America*. Washington, DC: Brookings Institution Press, 2013.

Korpi, Walter, and Joakim Palme. "The Paradox of Redistribution and Strategies of Equality: Welfare State Institutions, Inequality, and Poverty in the Western Countries." *American Sociological Review* (1998): 661–87.

Lau-Lavie, Amichai. "First Aid for Spiritual Seekers." *On Being*. Jul. 2017. Web 12 Aug. 2017.

Leo, Christopher, and Martine August. "The Multilevel Governance of Immigration and Settlement: Making Deep Federalism Work." *Canadian Journal of Political Science* 42.2 (2009): 491–510.

Lewis, Dan A., and Kendra P. Alexander. "United States." *The SAGE Encyclopedia of World Poverty*. Thousand Oaks: SAGE Publications, 2015, 1600–07.

Leygerman, Dina. "Poverty is a Choice, They Say." *Huffington Post*, 13 March 2017. Web. 12 Aug. 2017.

Lichter, Daniel T. "Poverty and Inequality Among Children." *Annual Review of Sociology* 23.1 (1997): 121–45.

Lietuva 2030. "Lithuania's Progress Strategy." Government of Lithuania, 2012.

Lindblom, Charles Edward. *Inquiry and Change.* New Haven: Yale University Press, 1990.

Lowi, Theodore J. "The Two Cities of Norton Long." *Cities Without Citizens*, Ed. Benjamin R. Schuster. Philadelphia: Center for the Study of Federalism, 1981.

Luhby, Tami. "America's Safety Net is at Risk from Trump's Budget Ax." CNN Money, 22 May 2017. Web. 12 Aug. 2017.

Lupia, Arthur, and Mathew D. McCubbins. *The Democratic Dilemma: Can Citizens Learn What They Need to Know?* Cambridge: Cambridge University Press, 1998.

Lynn Jr., Laurence E., Carolyn J. Heinrich, and Carolyn J. Hill. "Studying Governance and Public Management: Challenges and Prospects." *Journal of Public Administration Research and Theory* 10.2 (2000): 233–62.

MacLeod, Jay. *Ain't No Makin' It: Aspirations and Attainment in a Low-Income Neighborhood.* Boulder: Westview Press, 2009.

Mancilla, Alejandra. *The Right of Necessity: Moral Cosmopolitanism and Global Poverty.* London: Rowman & Littlefield, 2016.

Melish, Tara J. "Maximum Feasible Participation of the Poor: New Governance, New Accountability, and a 21st Century War on the Sources of Poverty." *Yale Human Rights and Development Journal*, 13.1 (2010): 1–134.

Miami Herald Editorial Board. "Florida's Democrats Still Act Like Losers." *Miami Herald*, 19 June 2017. Web. 12 Aug. 2017.

Michel, Edith F. Kauffer. "Leadership and Social Organization: The Integration of the Guatemalan Refugees in Campeche, Mexico." *Journal of Refugee Studies* 15.4 (2002): 359–87.

Miller, David. *Strangers in Our Midst: The Political Philosophy of Immigration.* Cambridge: Harvard University Press, 2016.

Miller, Alison L., Ronald Seifer, Laura Stroud, Stephen J. Sheinkopf, and Susan Dickstein. "Biobehavioral Indices of Emotion Regulation Relate to School Attitudes, Motivation, and Behavior Problems in a Low-Income Preschool Sample." *Annals of the New York Academy of Sciences* 1094.1 (2006): 325–29.

Milward, H. Brinton, and Keith G. Provan. "Governing the Hollow State." *Journal of Public Administration Research and Theory* 10.2 (2000): 359–80.

Montanaro, Laura. "The Democratic Legitimacy of Self-Appointed Representatives." *The Journal of Politics* 74.4 (2012): 1094–107.

Moynihan, Daniel P. "Maximum Feasible Misunderstanding; Community Action in the War on Poverty." 1969.

Musso, Juliet A., Christopher Weare, Nail Oztas, and William E. Loges. "Neighborhood Governance Reform and Networks of Community Power in Los Angeles." *The American Review of Public Administration* 36.1 (2006): 79–97.

Nabatchi, Tina, and Matt Leighninger. *Public Participation for 21st Century Democracy.* John Wiley & Sons, 2015.

Narayan-Parker, Deepa, and Raj Patel. *Voices of the Poor: Can Anyone Hear Us?* World Bank Publications, 2000.

Nawyn, Stephanie J. "Faith, Ethnicity, and Culture in Refugee Resettlement." *American Behavioral Scientist* 49.11 (2006): 1509–27.

Newsom, Gavin, and Lisa Dickey. *Citizenville: How to Take the Town Square Digital and Reinvent Government.* New York: The Penguin Press, 2013.

Office of Refugee Resettlement. United States Department of Health and Human Services. 2017. Web. 12 Aug. 2017.

O'Leary, Christopher J., Robert A. Straits, and Stephen A. Wandner. "U.S. Job Training: Types, Participants, and History." *W.E. Upjohn Institute for Employment Research,* 2004.

Osborne, David, and Ted Gaebler. *Reinventing Government: How the Entrepreneurial Spirit is Transforming Government.* Reading: Addison Wesley, 1993.

Oxfam. "An Economy for the 99%: It's Time to Build a Human Economy that Benefits Everyone, not Just the Privileged Few." *Oxfam Briefing Paper,* 2017.

Ozolina, Zaneta. *Societal Security: Inclusion-Exclusion Dilemma: A Portrait of the Russian-speaking Community in Latvia.* Zinatne, 2016.

Paletta, Damian. "Trump to Propose Big Cuts to Safety-Net in New Budget, Slashing Medicaid and Opening Door to Other Limits." *The Washington Post,* 21 May 2017. Web. 12 Aug. 2107.

Pimpare, Stephen. "Laziness Isn't Why People are Poor: And iPhones Aren't Why They Lack Health Care." *The Washington Post,* 8 March 2017. Web. 12 Aug. 2017.

Pittsburgh Foundation. "A Qualitative Study of Youth and the Juvenile Justice System: A 100 Percent Pittsburgh Pilot Project." 2017.

Pogge, Thomas. "Keynote Address: Poverty, Climate Change, and Overpopulation." *Ga. J. Int'l & Comp. L.* 38 (2009): 525.

Pop-Eleches, Grigore, and Joshua A. Tucker. *Communism's Shadow: Historical Legacies and Contemporary Political Attitudes.* Princeton: Princeton University Press, 2017.

Popkin, Susan J., Bruce Katz, Mary K. Cunningham, Karen D. Brown, Jeremy Gustafson, and Margery A. Turner. "A Decade of HOPE VI: Research Findings and Policy Challenges." *The Urban Institute,* 2004.

Prinz, Jesse L. "Is Empathy Necessary for Morality?" *Empathy: Philosophical and Psychological Perspecives.* Ed. Amy Coplan and Peter Goldie. Oxford: Oxford University Press, 2011.

Provan, Keith G., Mark A. Veazie, Lisa K. Staten, and Nicolette I. Teufel-Shone. "The Use of Network Analysis to Strengthen Community Partnerships." *Public Administration Review* 65.5 (2005): 603–13.

Provan, Keith G., Amy Fish, and Joerg Sydow. "Interorganizational Networks at the Network Level: A Review of the Empirical Literature on Whole Networks." *Journal of Management* 33.3 (2007): 479–516.

Rappaport, Nancy. "We are Overmedicating America's Poorest Kids." *The Washington Post*, 4 June 2014. Web. 12 Aug. 2017.

Ravallion, Martin. "The Idea of Antipoverty Policy." Working Paper 19210. *National Bureau of Economic Research*. 2013. Web. 12 Aug. 2017.

Reeves, Richard V. *Dream Hoarders: How the American Upper Middle Class is Leaving Everyone Else in the Dust, Why That Is a Problem, and What to Do about It.* Washington, DC: Brookings Institutions Press, 2017.

Richmond, Ted, and John Shields. "NGO-Government Relations and Immigrant Services: Contradictions and Challenges." *Journal of International Migration and Integration* 6.3–4 (2005): 513–26.

Riley-Smith, Tristram. *The Cracked Bell: America and the Afflictions of Liberty.* New York: Skyhorse Publishing, 2010.

Rosenblatt, Roger. "The Rugged Individual Rides Again." *Time*. October 15, 1984.

Rosenfeld, Raymond A., Laura A. Reese, Vicki Georgeau, and Scott Wamsley. "Community Development Block Grant Spending Revisited: Patterns of Benefit and Program Institutionalization." *Publius: The Journal of Federalism* 25.4 (1995): 55–72.

Royce, Edward. *Poverty and Power: The Problem of Structural Inequality.* Lanham: Rowman & Littlefield, 2015.

Salamon, Lester M. *The Tools of Government. A Guide to the New Governance.* New York: Oxford University Press, 2002.

Schmidt Sr, Ron. "Comparing Federal Government Immigrant Settlement Policies in Canada and the United States." *American Review of Canadian Studies* 37.1 (2007): 103–22.

Schneider, Anne L., and Helen M. Ingram. *Policy Design for Democracy.* Lawrence: University Press of Kansas, 1997.

Sen, Amartya. *Development as Freedom.* New York: Anchor Books, 1999.

Sherman, Jennifer. *Those Who Work, Those Who Don't: Poverty, Morality, and Family in Rural America.* Minneapolis: University of Minnesota Press, 2009.

Shields, John, Julie Drolet, and Karla Valenzuela. *Immigrant Settlement and Integration Services and the Role of Nonprofit Service Providers: A Cross-National Perspective on Trends, Issues and Evidence.* Ryerson Centre for Immigration and Settlement, 2016.

Sin Fronteras. 2017. Web. 12 Aug. 2017.

Sinkienė, Jolita, Eglė Gaulė, Jurgita Bruneckienė, Kęstutis Zaleckis, Thomas A. Bryer, and Evaldas Ramanauskas. "Interdisciplinary Perspectives on the Study of Vital Urban Communities." *Public Policy and Administration* 16.1 (2017): 9–23.

Skidelsky, Edward, and Robert Skidelsky. *How Much is Enough? Money and the Good Life.* Penguin UK, 2012.

Skocpol, Theda. *Diminished Democracy: From Membership to Management in American Civic Life.* Norman: University of Oklahoma Press, 2003.

Smeeding, Timothy M. "Multiple Barriers to Economic Opportunity for the 'Truly' Disadvantaged and Vulnerable." Russell Sage Foundation, 2016.

Smith, Kevin B., and Christopher W. Larimer. *The Public Policy Theory Primer*. Boulder: Westview Press, 2013.

Snyder, J. H. "Deterring Fake Public Participation." *International Journal of Public Participation* 4.1 (2010): 89–103.

Social Security Administration. "Historical Background and Development Security." 2017.

Somin, Ilya. "Creation, Consent, and Government Power over Property Rights." CATO Institute. 13 Dec. 2010. Web. 12 Aug. 2017. Accessed August 12, 2017.

Spiro, Gyorgy. *Captivity*. Brooklyn: Restless Books, 2015.

Sroufe, L. Alan. "Attachment and Development: A Prospective, Longitudinal Study from Birth to Adulthood." *Attachment & Human Development* 7.4 (2005): 349–67.

ST Lyrics. "When the Idle Poor Become the Idle Rich Lyrics—Finian's Rainbow Cast." 2017. Web. 18 Jan. 2018

Stassen, Martha L. "Student Outcomes: The Impact of Varying Living-Learning Community Models." *Research in Higher Education* 44.5 (2003): 581–613.

Stout, Jeffrey. *Blessed are the Organized: Grassroots Democracy in America*. Princeton: Princeton University Press, 2010.

Szewczyk-Sokolowski, Margaret, Kelly K. Bost, and Ada B. Wainwright. "Attachment, Temperament, and Preschool Children's Peer Acceptance." *Social Development* 14.3 (2005): 379–97.

Thomas, Paul. "Stop Blaming Poor Parents for their Children's Limited Vocabulary." *The Washington Post*, 10 Nov. 2014. Web. 12 Aug. 2017.

Trattner, Walter I. *From Poor Law to Welfare State: A History of Social Welfare in America*. New York: The Free Press, 1994.

Turner, Jonathan H., and Peter R. Turner. *The Structure of Sociological Theory*. New York: Wadsworth Publishing Company, 1998.

Underlid, Kjell. "Poverty and Experiences of Social Devaluation: A Qualitative Interview Study of 25 Long-Standing Recipients of Social Security Payments." *Scandinavian Journal of Psychology* 46 (2005): 273–83.

UNHCR. 2017. Web. 12 Aug. 2017.

United States Department of Agriculture. 2016. "Women, Infants and Children (WIC): About WIC." 2016. Web. 12 Aug. 2017.

———. "Supplemental Nutrition Assistance Program (SNAP)." 2017. Web. 12 Aug. 2017.

———. "Supplemental Nutrition Assistance Program (SNAP): A Short History of Snap." 2017. Web. 12 Aug. 2017.

United States Department of Health and Human Services. "Aid to Families with Dependent Children (AFDC) and Temporary Assistance for Needy Families (TANF) – Overview." 2009. Web. 12 Aug. 2017.

———. "History of Head Start." 2017. Web. 12 Aug. 2017.

United States Department of Housing and Urban Development. HOME and CDBG Guidebook. 2016. Web. 12 Aug. 2017.

————. 2017. "About HOPE VI." 2017. Web. 12 Aug. 2017.

United States Government Accountability Office. *The Distribution of Federal Economic Development Grants to Communities with High Rate of Poverty and Unemployment.* 2012.

————. *Community Development Block Grants: Sources of Data on Community Income are Limited.* 2016.

United States House of Representatives Republican Conference Task Force on Poverty, Opportunity, and Upward Mobility. "A Better Way: Our Vision for a Confident America: Poverty, Opportunity, and Upward Mobility." 2016. Web. 12 Aug. 2017.

United States Office of Management and Budget. *2018 Budget Blueprint to Make America Great Again.* 2017.

Venkatesh, Sudhir Alladi. *Off the Books: The Underground Economy of the Urban Poor.* Cambridge: Harvard University Press, 2006.

Walker, Robert, Grace Bantebya Kyomuhendo, Elaine Chase, and Sohail Choudhry. "Poverty in Global Perspective: Is Shame a Common Denominator?" *Journal of Social Policy* 42.2 (2013): 215–33.

Wang, XiaoHu, and Thomas A. Bryer. "Assessing the Costs of Public Participation: A Case Study of Two Online Participation Mechanisms." *The American Review of Public Administration* 43.2 (2013): 179–99.

Weizman, Z. O., and C. E. Snow. "Lexical Input as Related to Children's Vocabulary Acquisition: Effects of Sophisticated Exposure and Support for Meaning." *Developmental Psychology* 37.2 (2001): 265–79.

White, Brent T. "Underwater and Not Walking Away: Shame, Fear and the Social Management of the Housing Crisis." Arizona Legal Studies Discussion Paper No. 09–35. James E. Rogers College of Law, University of Arizona. 2009.

White House Neighborhood Revitalization Initiative. "The White House Neighborhood Revitalization Initiative." 2009. Web. 12 August 2017.

Wilson, Catherine E. "Collaboration of Nonprofit Organizations with Local Government for Immigrant Language Acquisition." *Nonprofit and Voluntary Sector Quarterly* 42.5 (2013): 963–84.

Wiltz, Teresa. "Without ID, Homeless Trapped in Vicious Cycle." PEW Charitable Trusts. 2017. Web. 12 Aug. 2017. analysis/blogs/stateline/2017/05/15/without-id-homeless-trapped-in-vicious-cycle

Wright, Robert G. "Voluntary Agencies and the Resettlement of Refugees." *International Migration Review* (1981): 157–74.

Young, Dennis R. "Nonprofit Management Studies in the United States: Current Developments and Future Prospects." *Journal of Public Affairs Education* (1999): 13–23.

Zimmerman, Marc A., and Julian Rappaport. "Citizen Participation, Perceived Control, and Psychological Empowerment." *American Journal of Community Psychology* 16.5 (1988): 725–50.

Index

~

About the Authors

Thomas Bryer, PhD, is a professor in the School of Public Administration and coordinator of the doctoral program in public affairs—public administration track within the College of Health and Public Affairs at the University of Central Florida. He is also a Fulbright scholar and a visiting professor at Kaunas University of Technology in Lithuania, and a visiting professor at the Institute for Public Policy and Professional Practice at Edge Hill University in the United Kingdom. He is the author of three additional books: *Higher Education beyond Job Creation: Universities, Communities, and Citizenship*; *National Service and Volunteerism: Achieving Impact in Our Communities*; and, *Social Media for Government: Theory and Practice* with Staci Zavattaro. He is also co-editor with Eglė Būtkevičienė of the Lexington Books series *Democratic Dilemmas and Policy Responsiveness*.

Sofia Prysmakova-Rivera is a PhD student studying public affairs within the College of Health and Public Affairs at the University of Central Florida. Over several years she has been working on a wide range of domestic and international projects in the areas of collaborative governance, civic engagement, migration, and poverty. She has presented her research at major national and international conferences, including European Group for Public Administration and American Society for Public Administration.

Made in the USA
Columbia, SC
07 January 2020